"This book is an extremely valuable addition not only to the growing library on IFS and specific topics, but also to the literature on how to work with grief. Audrey Davidheiser is a highly engaging writer who knows IFS well and includes clear examples (many from her personal experience) and ample experiential exercises. She is also well-versed in the research on grief and intersperses nuggets of wisdom from that literature throughout. This is a must read for Christian IFS therapists, for those who work with grief, and for non-Christian IFS therapists who have been put off by the exiling commands in the Bible."
Richard C. Schwartz, PhD, founder of Internal Family Systems Therapy

"Grief comes in waves that sometimes crash so hard it feels like they'll swallow us whole. Audrey Davidheiser helps us catch our breath, regain our bearings, swim safely to shore, and find the healing and wholeness we so desperately need. This is a fresh, innovative approach to grieving that will stretch you and help you breathe deeply again."
Margaret Feinberg, author of *The God You Need to Know*

"This is not a typical how-to book on navigating grief. Audrey's extensive knowledge and experience with IFS therapy, grounded in her strong foundation of Christian Scripture and faith, offer readers an opportunity for deep self-compassion, understanding, and healing."
Kathy Cox, lead trainer for the Internal Family Systems Institute

"As the title suggests, this book truly walks you through how to grieve wholeheartedly by utilizing the teachings of IFS therapy and providing practical exercises to help the reader work with and address each of their own grieving parts. Audrey Davidheiser's expertise in this therapy method, mingled with her incredible biblical knowledge, gives the reader the exact tools they need to face even the deepest forms of grief."
Tiffany Robbins, faith editor at Crosswalk.com

"I started reading this book shortly after the death of my maternal grandmother. I found myself taken over by thoughts that said that I didn't need to nor have time to grieve, and other parts that numbed me at the smallest expression of grief. This book helped me to identify this behavior and understand the challenges of grieving."
Tamala Floyd, author of *Listening When Parts Speak*

"Dr. Audrey Davidheiser provides a fresh perspective on the topic of grieving losses that will be helpful to a broad audience, especially to those who follow the Christian faith. The book is very practical and offers easy access to those who are grieving and involved in the integration of psychology and Christian faith. Dr. Davidheiser is very transparent in this book and directly addresses her own grief and loss. In this way she models for the reader how to grieve in a helpful manner that brings healing. By describing the Internal Family Systems (IFS) model, she breaks new ground in this important and universal experience of grief."
Clark D. Campbell, former dean of Rosemead School of Psychology

"Having grown up in the church and being a firm believer in the resurrection of life through faith in Jesus Christ, I was shocked to learn how ill-equipped I was to grieve after I saw my mother draw her last breath. Through her compassionate book, Audrey Davidheiser poured a soothing balm on my soul as she walked me through the process of mourning this traumatic loss."
Cindi McMenamin, author of *When God Sees Your Tears*

"*Grieving Wholeheartedly* offers compassionate and practical support for Christians navigating the complex landscape of grief. Drawing from the transformational Internal Family Systems model, Audrey Davidheiser invites readers to embrace their inner parts and find healing through God's love. A beautiful read for anyone seeking to understand their grief in a deeper and more holistic way."
Jenna Riemersma, author and certified Internal Family Systems therapist

"Grief and loss are universal experiences that are often fraught with difficulty and struggle. Audrey Davidheiser's ways of sharing her own journey with grief, while acknowledging and honoring the uniqueness of each individual's experiences, creates a space that welcomes all the different parts of us that are activated in the grieving process."
Ellie Cunanan-Petty, assistant trainer for the IFS Institute

"Audrey Davidheiser's credentials, writing finesse, and experience offer a gracious, literary path of healing, encouraging us to accept grief's unavoidable presence but to walk through the bleakness with bold fervor, trusting beams of hope and love to light the way home."
Peyton Garland, editor of iBelieve.com

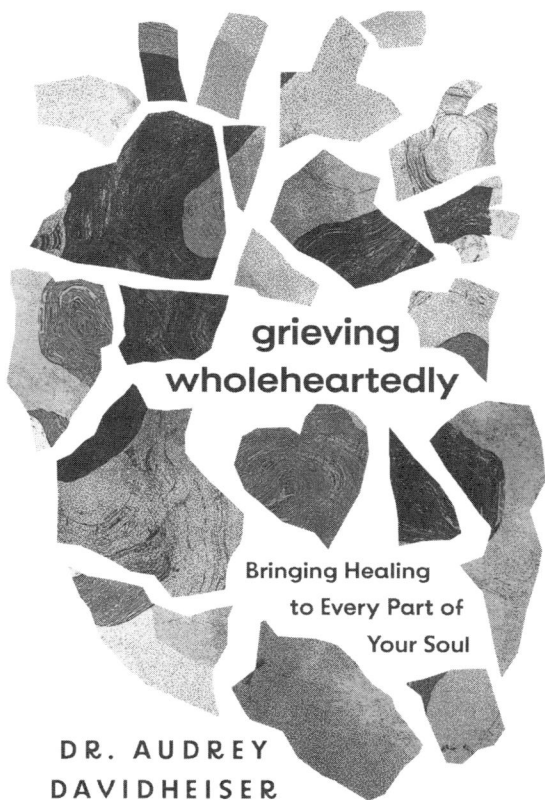

grieving wholeheartedly

Bringing Healing to Every Part of Your Soul

DR. AUDREY DAVIDHEISER

ĩvp

An imprint of InterVarsity Press
Downers Grove, Illinois

InterVarsity Press
P.O. Box 1400 | Downers Grove, IL 60515-1426
ivpress.com | email@ivpress.com

InterVarsity Press® is the publishing division of InterVarsity Christian Fellowship/USA®. For more information, visit intervarsity.org.

All Scripture quotations, unless otherwise indicated, are taken from The Holy Bible, New International Version®, NIV®. Copyright © 1973, 1978, 1984, 2011 by Biblica, Inc.™ Used by permission of Zondervan. All rights reserved worldwide. www.zondervan.com. The "NIV" and "New International Version" are trademarks registered in the United States Patent and Trademark Office by Biblica, Inc.™

While any stories in this book are true, some names and identifying information may have been changed to protect the privacy of individuals.

Family photos: Audrey Davidheiser

Author is represented by the literary agency of Credo Communications LLC, Grand Rapids, MI, www.credocommunications.net.

The publisher cannot verify the accuracy or functionality of website URLs used in this book beyond the date of publication.

Cover design: Faceout Studio, Spencer Fuller
Interior design: Daniel van Loon
Images: © GeorgePeters / DigitalVision Vectors via Getty Images, © oxygen / Moment via Getty Images

ISBN 978-1-5140-1083-9 (print) | ISBN 978-1-5140-1084-6 (digital)

Printed in the United States of America ∞

Library of Congress Cataloging-in-Publication Data
A catalog record for this book is available from the Library of Congress.

32   31   30   29   28   27   26   25 | 13   12   11   10   9   8   7   6   5   4   3   2   1

FOR PAPA

Palembang, October 23, 1948–Jakarta, July 14, 2018

I thank my God for all the memories I have of you.

Philippians 1:3 GW

Contents

Grieving Affects Your Parts

ONLY TWO TYPES OF PEOPLE EXIST. Those who have buried a loved one—and those who will. Since you are here, I assume you identify with the first category. The one prior to the dash. Pre-dash. Before someone dear departed and dashed your heart.

Who died? Your spouse? Fiancée? Maybe you lost a child to suicide. A friend to a freak accident. Or maybe you had to put your beloved pet to sleep.

It is also possible to mourn something other than physical death—a relational rupture (divorce, broken engagement, psychological trauma), financial hardship (job termination, a house fire), and losing your health or mobility can also culminate in grief. But perhaps your loss is more ambiguous in that there is no closure. You fit this description if you have been caring for a relative with a degenerative disease or if your loved one went missing.

Different details shroud our losses, but one similarity unites our suffering: death affects our soul and its parts. Whatever it was that brought you here, welcome.

In the past, I would have mumbled my condolences only to comply with societal norms. All was relatively well because the two people who bequeathed me everything—down to their DNA—still shared the same air I breathed. I could call them night or day and despite their flaws, and my faults and our fusses, both parents had my back. Those days found me frolicking on the right side of the dash.

But then death snatched my father, smothering me with an acrid reality: neither an MA in theology nor a PhD in clinical psychology immunized me from grief. There is no insider special for mental health professionals to skip their own grieving. I had to experience what other mourners have discovered—losing your beloved feels like sprouting a hole in your heart that stays gaping, throbbing with pain, its ache transmitting a wordless warning: *everything may look similar, but nothing is the same—now that your person is forever gone.*

In light of this firsthand bout with grieving, I am extending sincere sorrow for your loss.

WHAT TO EXPECT

Grief comes from an old Latin root *gravāre*, which carries the sense of weight and heaviness (think "gravity.") No wonder grieving feels burdensome, tempting us to try and sidestep our feelings. The PhD in me can specify sound reasons why it is fine to sob because I miss my dad. And yet, other parts of me strive to avert the waterworks. But if a psychologist feels this way, I can imagine a layperson's resistance to wholeheartedly grieve.

Thankfully, Internal Family Systems (IFS) can help. This therapeutic model recognizes we grieve differently from one another—but so do different parts of our souls. This is why the same loss can induce multiple reactions. For instance, a sibling who mourns the death of her brother might blame him for driving while intoxicated. But sweet childhood memories force her to weep over his senseless death—which causes another part to feel aggrieved by this (soggy) show of sentiment.

Most books on grief utilize a unitary lens. They package the author's thoughts into a memoir, devotional, or series of lessons on the nature of grief. However, approaching grief through a solitary lens will benefit some—but not all—parts. We cannot assume all our parts need the exact same things before they release their grief-related burdens. IFS provides a pathway to help our whole soul grieve, including parts of us that are in conflict with each other.

Consider this book like the Pixar movie *Inside Out*—but for mourners.[1]

BOOK OVERVIEW

Starting with the fundamentals of grieving and IFS is the theme of the first section. Chapter one builds a case for why—as unpleasant as it is—we cannot afford to avoid grieving. Chapter two focuses on the primary principles behind IFS: everyone has a Self and parts. Chapter three invites us to consider the compatibility of IFS with Christianity by showcasing passages from the Old and New Testaments that reveal multiplicity in the Bible.

Think of the second part of the book as the Land of Protectors. We will not gain a wholehearted access to our more vulnerable parts (also known as "exiles") unless we first meet with our "protector" parts. The chapters here collectively demonstrate how to negotiate with our own protectors, so please read this section in its entirety—even if you do not identify with all the protectors listed there.

In chapter four, we learn why getting permission from our protectors is key. The chapter will also teach us how to discern and identify different parts, particularly those affected by our loss. The next two chapters introduce us to important manager parts: thinking parts and inner critics (chapter five), followed by religious parts (chapter six). Getting to know these stalwart manager parts is imperative, because although they mean well, they can also appear heartless in their efforts to shield us from the messiness of grief.

Next up is a class of protectors called "firefighters." These parts will do whatever it takes to divert our attention from emotional pain. Firefighters employ many strategies to extinguish our pain, but chapter seven will focus on distractions, soothing substances (alcohol, fried food, sugar), as well as dissociation and numbness.

The third part of the book honors the uniqueness of each mourner. Because each loss is unique, you are welcome to read only the chapters that fit your particular circumstance. Altogether, you will find help for vulnerable parts that hold shock (chapter eight), sadness and sorrow (chapter nine), anger and rage (chapter ten), guilt and regret (chapter eleven), fear (chapter twelve), and loneliness (chapter thirteen).

The final section prepares us for the future. Chapter fourteen provides guidance on what to do with parts we have not covered in this book, as well as suggestions on how to fortify our internal systems in light of future birthdays, anniversaries, and major holidays. Chapter fifteen offers a glimpse on how our life might look after we grieve wholeheartedly.

DIPPING INSIDE

Since we are applying IFS to the grieving process, you can expect excerpts of actual IFS sessions from real clients. But I am also committed to safeguarding my clients' confidentiality. Therefore, I have altered their gender, ethnicity, age, and other identifying markers by which they might have been recognized. In some cases I also combined details from various clients to present a composite sketch.

As helpful as reading about someone else's IFS breakthrough may be, though, it is still eons away from experiencing it yourself. For this reason, you will have the chance to work with your parts in the Dipping Inside segments. You can almost think of these exercises as working with your own IFS therapist.

Proverbs 16:24 reveals there is power within winsome words: "Gracious words are a honeycomb, sweet to the soul and healing to the bones." Because there are no more gracious words than the Almighty's, Bible verses are peppered throughout this book for the benefit of you and your parts.

But that brings us to a somber reality. Church hurt *is* real. Some with religiously savvy parts have wielded God's Word against folks like us and used their authority to impose their (perverse) will on us. If you have religious or spiritual trauma, I am so sorry. It makes sense for you to view this book with suspicion.

I address grief (and IFS) from a Christian perspective because I can only write from experience—and it was relentless Love (1 John 4:8, 16) who sustained me through many hardships, including the untimely death of my father. Regardless of your spiritual background, however, you are welcome here. I prayerfully wrote this book in the hope of alleviating your burden. May its pages offer you ease, and spaciousness, to work with your parts.

Grieving is as universal as it is unwanted. If we cannot break our appointment with grief, let's approach it with gentleness.

Will you join me?

PART 1

Fundamentals

1

Grieving

UNWANTED, YET UNAVOIDABLE

I HATE GRIEVING.

There. I said it.

A part of me did, actually. The part that abhors the tears I shed while writing this book.

But I am not the only one with parts. Your soul comes pre-packaged with them too. Have you noticed the maelstrom of reactions following your loss? Perhaps maintaining concentration has been hard, as your mind keeps slipping to memories of the deceased or fears about tomorrow. Your digestive system feels wonky. Reminders of your loss spur shame, guilt, perhaps even both. Maybe you avoid crying at all costs. These are some of the ways your parts might have expressed themselves.

Grief intrudes differently into our existence. Did you sense death's steady cadence as cancer colonized your sweetheart bit by bit? Or did the grave ambush someone you loved? My initiation to the world of grieving fit the latter category. On July 2, 2018, I waved goodbye to my parents as they boarded a jet to Jakarta, Indonesia, after spending their summer stateside.

My dad died less than two weeks later.

You will read about my shock and the deep sorrow that followed suit in later chapters. For now, it is enough to say his sudden departure shoved me into a surreal world. Sleep spurned me that first night. I dialed my mom three times instead, driven by the intense urge to hear her voice—the least I could do, given the thousands of miles tearing me from her embrace.

One thought kept looping back in between reliving memories of the last time I saw him: *I can't believe he's gone.*

Even when sleep eventually returned, I often awoke with a start. Fear fueled my dreams. Day and night I battled the dread that my mom's broken heart would soon finish her off.

Denial accompanied my dazed state. One day I spotted my father at the local hardware store. I ran through the aisles to glimpse him—but of course, it was just a random man with a similar build as his. Another day, I heard his footsteps by our bedroom. Except it was just my bittersweet memory from when my father had fetched us Saturday breakfast from the farmer's market.

His death disoriented me. I had always assumed my parents would grow old and retire together. Losing my father made me sad, but also mad: *How come others my age still have both their parents but I can't?*

I could not string *my dad* and *dead* in the same sentence for the first year after he passed. To do so would have cemented as reality the awful situation I loathed.

GRIEF'S INDIVIDUALIZED IMPACT

Elizabeth Kübler-Ross postulated grief as passing in five stages—denial, anger, bargaining, depression, and acceptance.[1] Prior to her own death, however, Kübler-Ross clarified her position: "[The stages] were never meant to help tuck messy emotions into neat packages. They are responses to loss that many people have, but there is not a typical response to loss, as there is no typical loss."[2]

Even with her own admission, and even though the scientific community has debunked the stage theory of grief, many still cling to the stubborn belief that grieving progresses in a tidy trajectory.[3] But prescribing the same neat steps for mourners everywhere is as realistic as restricting every Disneyland visitor to only a handful of rides, with a specific order to boot.

Truth is, many factors determine how we approach loss. Our psychological composition, faith tradition, family background, culture, and upbringing all play significant roles. Whether we have fully dealt with prior losses can also determine how our current grief fares. If we repressed or glossed over past losses, for example, the current emotional load might tip us over—which might then activate the impulse to get high, work overtime, super-spiritualize grief, or engage in other strategies to smother our emotions.

Our history with the deceased and circumstances around that death will also influence how we grieve. An abused teenager is unlikely to mourn her stepfather's death; and if her mother was clueless about his harmful behavior, the mother's grief might incite her to lash out at the teen for appearing aloof. The grandkids whose grandmother spoiled them before dementia took over might be wrecked with sorrow. But their mother—who quit her job to take care of her mom—might feel secretly relieved to be liberated from heavy caretaking responsibilities.

Regardless of how others do it, you are free to mourn in your own way. The same goes for each part of your soul.

UNPROCESSED GRIEF'S FATAL CONSEQUENCE

King Solomon once made an interesting comparison: "Love is as strong as death" (Song of Solomon 8:6). How strong? Death can rip marriages apart, such as when parents blame each other after their child dies. When the deceased leaves a substantial will that is then contested, death can also pit family members against one another.

In the case of suicide, its imprint can be indelible in the soul of those psychologically close to the deceased. A suicide can deposit in survivors increased risks of killing themselves.[4] This grim prediction proved true in my personal world. My husband, John, and I befriended a man who, as a young adult, discovered his mother's body after her suicide. This sensitive soul wound up with chronic depression and tried to mimic her exit strategy several times throughout his adulthood. He eventually took his own life in his late 70s.

Death *is* formidable.

What may be less obvious is the equally powerful potential of unprocessed grief. Consider Moses' story in the Old Testament for example. Numbers chapter 20 opens with the breaking news of Miriam's death. She was Moses' older sister who also rescued him from infanticide (Exodus 2:1-9). No doubt this childhood history hovered in Moses' mind when he learned about her passing. Her death must have affected him.

But did he have the space to grieve? Not if the rest of the clan could help it. They were too consumed by their own need to let Moses attend to his—much less slip him a sympathy card or home-cooked meal. Miriam died in an arid place, and no matter where the Israelites dug, they could not find a drop of water anywhere.

Out came the complaints.

Study the Torah—the first five books of the Hebrew Bible—and you will see there is nothing unusual about their response to this latest trial. The Israelites grumbled their way throughout the forty-year sojourn in the desolate wilderness. In a way, their discontentment is understandable. They were already saddled with the generational trauma of being enslaved. Then they had to surrender the only home they knew—Egypt—for an endless trek across the vast desert day after day (after day). But to do so while dehydrated?

Ask anyone who has felt "hangry" and they might admit it: hunger can easily drive you to complain. And so can thirst. "My baby is *parched*, Moses. She's been crying nonstop since our last camp, but there's no oasis anywhere. She needs to drink!"

How Moses responded made the moment memorable. The Almighty had informed Moses to grab his staff, gather everyone around a giant rock, and speak to it. The inanimate object would then gush water (Numbers 20:7-8). But this transpired instead: "[Moses] and Aaron summoned the people to come and gather at the rock. 'Listen, you rebels!' he shouted. 'Must we bring you water from this rock?' Then Moses raised his hand and struck the rock twice with the staff, and water gushed out. So the entire community and their livestock drank their fill" (Numbers 20:10-11 NLT).

Hallelujah! Problem solved.

But did you notice how the story diverged from God's decree? God told Moses to *speak* to the rock; Moses *struck* it instead. Can't you see Moses standing there, seething under the shadeless sun, swallowing raw grief because the people only care about themselves? No wonder he thwacked the rock in frustration.

But the man the Bible describes as "a very humble man, more humble than anyone else on the face of the earth" (Numbers 12:3) also *shouted* at the crowd. Humble people do not typically raise their voice. A humble man who feels overwhelmed, however, might.

File that tidbit away as we review what he said next. "Must we [as in Moses and Aaron] bring you water from this rock?"

Whoa, Moses. Did you just take credit for the miracle?

The turn of events provoked the Almighty. "But the LORD said to Moses and Aaron, 'Because you did not trust in me enough to honor me as holy in the sight of the Israelites, you will not bring this community into the land I give them'" (Numbers 20:12).

Let's zoom out of the dusty desert scene to reflect. Moses' track record shows a consistent trend of applying patience to pacify his people's demands (for instance, Exodus 14:10-14; Exodus 15:22-25; Exodus 16:1-8; Exodus 17:1-6; Numbers 11:1-3; and Numbers 14:1-20). Yet the one time he lost composure happened on the heels of his sister's death.

Coincidence? Doubtful—and let me explain why.

Soon after Miriam died, Moses' remaining sibling, Aaron, followed suit. Notice what happened next: "All the Israelites mourned for him thirty days" (Numbers 20:29). Yet, the Bible makes no similar mention following Miriam's passing. There was no eulogy for her. No national day of mourning. No space for the masses—much less Moses—to mourn her departure.

I submit it was the lack of space to grieve the loss of his sister that drove Moses to disobey the Lord *and* steal his glory. God showed Moses his ways (Psalm 103:7) and talked to him in person (Exodus 33:11). He entrusted Moses with the Ten Commandments— twice (Exodus 19:20–20:17; Exodus 34:1-33). But neither Moses' intimacy with God, nor his pivotal position in Judaism and Christianity alike, exempted Moses from the emotional task of mourning.

The man God handpicked to marshal his multitude into their destiny (Exodus 3:1–4:16) ended up missing his own—likely due to a death he did not fully mourn. If spiritual giants cannot afford to bypass grieving, neither can we.

GRIEVING BENEFITS YOU

Missing our destiny may be a steep price for skipping grief, but it is not the only one. There are also physical and emotional costs to consider.

Elyce Wakerman's father died from a heart attack when she was only 3. Her book *Father Loss* reveals how Wakerman appraised this early loss as affecting everything she did. Small wonder she felt compelled to study the impact of fatherlessness on daughters, whether because of death, divorce, or abandonment. Reflecting on the results of her pilot study, Wakerman concludes, "Unresolved grief may result in unexplainable sadness, defenses against emotional commitment, or the very serious condition of denying feelings altogether."[5] Unacknowledged grief frequently appears as a chronic state of apathy.

But that is not all. Failure to process grief can also undermine health. According to professor Toni Miles, who completed a statewide survey of bereavement in Georgia in 2019, binge drinking increased in the bereaved individuals in her study.[6] Miles cautioned how grief may cause mourners to neglect wearing seat belts, pick up their old smoking habit, or stop taking care of their medical needs.[7]

A scent, a melody, a specific time of day, something someone says—*anything* can trigger your grief. Please make room for your feelings when these tender moments materialize. Rather than avoiding them, how about viewing the loss in your life as an invitation to venture into your internal world, where emotions reside?

DIPPING INSIDE

What came up for you in this chapter? Jot down every thought, feeling, and sensation you noticed. For instance, if you resonated with the part of me that resented grieving, write it down. Reactions you note down in this section likely represent parts of your soul.

Now, consider the loss that brought you to this book. Are you noticing any resistance to grieving that loss? If so, listen to what the thought says and write it down fully.

_____

_____

_____

_____

Let the part of you that resists grieving know that you hear it.

Did you sense any response from the inside? For instance, you might sense an inaudible *thanks*. Jot it down too.

_____

_____

_____

_____

_____

If there are any reactions to this chapter you have not written down, you can do it now.

_____

_____

_____

_____

_____

Thank every part that showed up.

From childhood until he left, my father always supported me (Jakarta, Indonesia)

The Abcs of IFS

THIS HAS NEVER HAPPENED BEFORE.

I was sitting in a continuing education (CE) course when the thought scrolled through my mind. As a licensed psychologist, I had to fulfill the Board of Psychology's requirements to renew my license every two years. By then I had memorized the script surrounding the process: register; pay for the course; show up; learn something worthwhile—though probably not life-changing—to justify the money and time spent.

Carrying my tote and this expectation, I scooted into my seat as Dr. Frank Anderson introduced Internal Family Systems (IFS) to the audience. He explained the model's basic principles before instructing participants to pair up for a five-minute exercise. I took the role of "therapist" first, practicing the rudimentary IFS skills he had just taught.

When I switched roles with my partner and became her "client," those two and a half minutes sparked an irreversible domino effect. All my "therapist" did was read the prompts on the course handout. She followed the standard IFS protocol, nothing fancy. Yet, as she did, something percolated within me.

I sensed resentment against myself.

Later on I realized how the sentiment was a reaction from my parts, who let me know in no uncertain terms how they resented my outward focus. This is what they meant: by the time the internal incident at the CE course happened, I had practiced as a licensed psychologist for a decade; tack on another five years of providing therapy under supervision, and it pushed the number to fifteen long years of paying attention to my clients and their presenting problems—the world outside.

My parts took this to mean I was available to everyone except for them.

Sadly, they were right. No wonder they resented me!

That unforgettable experience launched my IFS journey. Those 150 seconds so moved me that I snapped up any opportunity to attend more IFS trainings. After hearing Dr. Richard Schwartz present in a two-day workshop, I signed up for all three levels of formal IFS training, worked with my own IFS therapist, became certified in the model, and earned official approval by the IFS Institute as a consultant.

I learned to befriend my internal world.

DR. RICHARD SCHWARTZ

Dr. Schwartz—or Dick, as he is fondly known in the IFS world—stumbled on the Internal Family Systems model in the 1980s, while working as a family therapist trained in the prevailing family systems theories of the day.[1] Despite his status as the founder of a major therapy approach, Dick comes across as humble and accessible. In the last IFS training I attended, for instance, Dick engaged with long lines of IFS aficionados in between workshop sessions. He indulged participants who sought his autograph, picture, or clinical wisdom—sometimes all three. Dick's relatability is truly refreshing.

But back to the early days of IFS. As Dick listened to his clients, he discovered a curious phenomenon: they seemed to have a natural ability to relate to the parts that made up their internal systems. The more Dick swapped his preconceived notions about psychology for his clients' descriptions of their inner worlds, the more he learned about the fascinating ways in which the soul operates.

Today, IFS is not only one of the fastest growing therapy approaches in the world,[2] it is also rated as evidence-based. A growing body of research is supporting its efficacy in treating mental illness—which includes PTSD,[3] phobia, panic, GAD, and depressive symptoms.[4]

You are invited to embark on the same internal journey Dick embraced decades ago.

PARTS AND SELF

Consider all the skills required to read a book cover to cover. At minimum, the alphabet. Mastering these letters has to happen before a child can learn to decipher the meaning of words, phrases, idioms, and eventually, whole books. Nobody can appreciate Jane Austen's *Pride and Prejudice* without sinking thousands of hours into many simpler proses first. If we compare an IFS session to reading a book, starting with the ABCs of the theory is mandatory. That would be the existence of parts and Self (intentionally capitalized).

Parts. These members of our soul—also known as "subpersonalities"—have their own reactions to our experience. Their presence explains why we can sprout a variety of responses to the same topic. For instance, a part of you may nod along as you read on, another part might exude skepticism, and yet another part may be ruminating about something else altogether.

Having multiple parts within our soul is *not* pathological. Multiplicity is a trait every person possesses. If the idea of having sub-personalities feels unnerving, however, you are welcome to view it differently—like considering "parts" as different "aspects" of yourself. For instance, consider how the version of you who strives for promotion at work is different than the playful one who tickles your kids, who is also different than the snappy one who shows up when an irresponsible driver cuts you off on the freeway.

You can also think of parts as metaphorical. Or you can consider parts to be a creative or imaginative way to describe your inner system, similar to Riley's different emotions in *Inside Out*.

Parts can manifest visually—not because you are hallucinating, but because you see them in your mind's eye. Some people see their parts as shapes, like a blob, stick figure, or small ball. Others see their parts as different colors (like *Inside Out*'s Sadness being blue and Anger being red.)

Regardless of how you conceptualize parts, learning about them will benefit you. That's because your parts are, well, a part of who you are. Getting to know these key players in your inner world will enlighten you on how your internal system operates. A simple way to start is by tuning into your mind; if you eavesdrop on your own stream of consciousness, what do you "hear" there?

For instance, if Mother's Day is approaching and you are out shopping, your inner chatter might sound like the following: *Did I turn off the stove before leaving? I sure hope so. Let's just find a gift for Mom and skedaddle. Hey, that's a nice blouse! Does it come in her size?* Schwartz suggested, "All of us are born with many sub-minds that are constantly interacting inside of us. This is in general what we call thinking, because the parts are talking to each other and to you constantly about things you have to do or debating the best course of action, and so on."[5] The next time you have a thought, therefore, pause. Ask inside, *Which part said that?*

Martha Sweezy, another senior IFS trainer, defines the *psyche* (that is, our soul) as "a meeting place for the many opinions and perspectives of their parts."[6] By befriending your inner system, you will develop the ability to detect whether you are hearing from one part or more.

Frank Anderson—the instructor of my life-changing CE course—explained in his book *Transcending Trauma* how parts can utilize our body to communicate.[7] The next time you feel physical sensations (rapid breathing, clammy hands, tense shoulders, tingling sensations, and so on), focus on that sensation and be curious. Ask inside: *Is a part trying to tell me something through this sensation? If so, may we please convert this conversation into English* (or another language you are fluent in)?

Parts can also appear in the form of feelings, such as loneliness, longing, or jealousy; beliefs can come from a part; the same goes with memory. And what about dreams? Scripture says dreams can come from God (see Genesis 37:5-11; Genesis 41:1-36; Daniel 7; Matthew 1:18-24; 2:13-23; Acts 2:17). Since God never changes (Hebrews 13:8), we can still expect him to fill our sleep with messages from above. But dreams can also be the product of our own soul (Ecclesiastes 5:3). Soul-level dreams happen when parts direct the screenplay. Because they are content creators, parts can infiltrate the night seasons with messages for us, as well as their fears and wishes. For the bereaved, dreaming about the one we lost is typical.[8]

Table 2.1. Common Terms in IFS

IFS Term	Definition	Example
Blending/blended	The phenomenon when a part merges its perspective, emotion, beliefs, and impulses with us, causing us to feel, think, and behave the way it does.[9]	If an angry part is blended with you, you will feel anger at your spouse for dying and leaving you alone.

IFS Term	Definition	Example
Unblending/unblended	The condition when a part agrees to create internal space for us, allowing us to feel our own feelings.	Once you are unblended from the angry part, you may feel curious about why this part is so angry.
Burden	Restrictive emotions, beliefs, and memories that are carried by burdened parts.	A vulnerable part (that the angry part protects) believes your spouse died because everyone eventually leaves, because the vulnerable part is so unworthy of love.
Unburdening	The process by which a burdened part can release its burden.	Once the vulnerable part receives your and God's love for it, this part releases its belief about being unlovable.

But of all the ways we can recognize a part, *blending* is perhaps the easiest way to do so (see table 2.1). That is because when a part is blended with us, we feel what that particular part feels. So if you are blended with a self-doubting part, you will be consumed with the hesitancy and insecurity originating from this part. If a controlling part is blended with you, you will insist on having your husband text you when he will leave work and whether he will fill up the car or drop by anywhere else before heading home, because knowing his precise ETA means you can avoid worst-case scenarios—*Why isn't he here yet?*—playing on a loop, terrifying you senseless.

Don't, uh, ask me how I know.

Here is a more tangible example of what it means to be blended with a part of your soul. Imagine holding an agitated toddler in your lap. After a while, you will feel somewhat anxious too, just by virtue of your proximity with the energetic child, right? Likewise with being blended with a part.

Self. Your Self is the you who is not a part. Your Self is unharmed from whatever happened in your past. It is the real you, born equipped with the God-given qualities known in IFS as the "8 C's" (see table 2.2).[10]

Table 2.2. The 8 C's of Self

Characteristics of the Self	Definition
Courageous	The ability to take complete responsibility for your actions and make amends to correct your errors; the willingness to reflect upon and explore your inner world.
Compassionate	To be open-heartedly present and appreciative of others and your Self without feeling the urge to fix, change, distance, or judge.
Calm	The ability to react to triggers in your environment in less automatic and extreme ways.
Confidence	The ability to stay fully present in a situation and effectively handle or repair anything that happens.
Clarity	The ability to perceive situations accurately without distortion from extreme beliefs and emotions.
Creativity	The use of the imagination to produce original ideas; the ability to enter the "flow state" in which expression spontaneously flows out of you and you are immersed in the pleasure of the activity.
Connectedness	The ability to relax your defenses with others as you know you won't be judged or controlled; to have companionship and/or spirituality that helps you deal with reality in a way that transcends circumstances.
Curiosity	A strong desire to know or learn something new about a topic, situation, or person in a non-judgmental way; to have a sense of wonder about the world and how things work.

I once attended a workshop in which an audience member inquired why Self characteristics excluded love. Dick quipped, "Because love doesn't start with the letter C." Dick might have been joking, but as you will see in chapter three, Self embodies qualities that Christians recognize to be Christlike. When your Self is in charge, you will feel one of these 8 C's qualities—regardless of how challenging your circumstance is.

What if you do not, or cannot, feel any of the 8 C's?

It does *not* mean you don't have a Self. Rather, a part is likely blended with you. Since a loud noise always overpowers quieter ones, when we are blended with a part, we also notice the insistent feelings and thoughts of that part. This condition obscures the "quieter" state of being calm or any of the 8 C's.

As an example, working with extreme protector parts has intimidated some of my parts. Thoughts like *saying the wrong thing would upset this person—yikes!* entered my mind. But once I asked my parts to allow me (that is, my Self) to lead, and if they relented, I would be able to navigate through any session confidently. There have been times when, after my parts unblended, I said something I had never thought before—which my client, or a participant in an IFS training, validated to be what they needed to hear. That is because when my Self is leading, I have a clear connection with God, who alone possesses the secrets of wisdom (Job 11:6).

Another indication that your Self is present is when you exude genuine warmth regardless of how the other party presents. This is true whether you are relating with people on the outside or parts on the inside.

HOW PARTS RESPOND

Just as parts manifest in a number of different ways, they can also react in a variety of ways. This is why it is not enough to only cultivate an awareness of your parts; it is also crucial to communicate to them and acknowledge their response.

When you engage your parts with an open heart, you may notice relief or relaxation as a result. For instance, if you counter the throbbing pain in the base of your skull by sending compassion there, do not be surprised when the pain dissipates. If you ask for space and a part agrees, you might feel more relaxed because of it.

Parts can also respond through thoughts. This is no different than the typical banter you hear within yourself.

You: *Where did I misplace my ring?*

Critical part: *Great. That heirloom was from your late mom, right? How can you be so careless?*

Angry part: *Be quiet! You think judging her will help?*

Have you heard a similar back and forth in your own mind? The next time you do, try responding like this: *Hey Anger, thanks for defending me. Critical part, would you like to help me be more organized? Let's find that ring together.*

Want to hear a live reaction from my system? I sensed astonishment emanating from my own critical part as I typed the last paragraph—as though this part never imagined I would ask it for help. I disclose this reaction to show how our parts can interact with us at any given moment. Even though the skit on the missing ring *is* fictitious, my inner critic paid enough attention to the point that it reacted immediately to what I was doing.

DO PARTS LIE?

You can dialogue with your parts and expect them to respond honestly. Does that mean parts tell the truth? In my experience, yes. Parts do not enjoy carrying heavy burdens. They yearn to be unburdened and will do whatever it takes, including baring their soul, if it means relief is afoot. This eagerness to eliminate pain motivates them to tell the truth.

Still, if in your own internal journey you find yourself wondering if a part is telling a white lie, you can clarify. Ask the part something like, *Are you responding this way because you think you should? Are you telling me what you think I want to hear?* Assure your part you can handle the whole truth, no matter how ugly it is.

When you are unsure, you can ask the Spirit of Truth whether the part you are talking to is telling you the whole truth (John 16:13). The truth will eventually emerge. Always.

CATEGORIES OF PARTS

There are three categories of parts: exiles, managers, and firefighters (see table 2.3).

Table 2.3. Three Types of Parts in IFS

	Managers*	Firefighters*	Exiles
Who	Proactive protector parts	Reactive protector parts	Vulnerable parts carrying burdens
Job description	Internally, to shield us from getting in touch with exiles. Externally, managers strive to exert as much control as possible.	To rescue us from emotional pain using any means necessary. Firefighters take over when triggers activate exiles and flood our awareness with emotional pain.	Exiles do not have a job in the internal world. However, they aspire to be freed from their burdens.
Examples	Parts whose jobs are to: criticize (ourselves and others) think/analyze make and/or save money follow rules be perfect please people rescue, fix, or caretake focus on physical image overwork control ruminate	Parts that prompt us to: rest/relax resort to humor travel use addictive substances be distracted overeat do risky behavior consider suicide dissociate feel numb sleep	Parts that feel or believe they are: shameful worthless abandoned rejected hopeless unlovable helpless lonely forgotten needy invisible unwanted overlooked

*Protectors (or protector parts) refer to both managers and firefighters.

Exiles are hurt parts that carry vulnerable feelings, memories, and beliefs. For instance, Joannie's husband had been hiding an affair with a woman half his age. When Joannie confronted him about it, he filed for divorce, leaving her with an exile who believed *he left me because I'm not good enough.*

Managers and *firefighters* are considered protector parts. Their mission? To shield us from our exiles' threatening feelings and beliefs. They will do whatever it takes to protect us from reliving the humiliation or trauma from yesteryear. But their strategies vary. Manager parts accomplish this goal by being proactive in controlling our behavior. For instance, the manager that oversees my finances insists on unplugging unused appliances and prompts me to hunt for bargains, all to save money. There is also a hardworking manager that criticizes me daily, with the hopes that this valiant effort at self-improvement would deter others from disparaging me.

Other common managers include parts that prompt us to be punctual, in control, intellectual, perfect, follow rules, blend with the background, please others, police our looks. All managers share the same two objectives: to keep things predictable and safe in the external world *and* to banish our exiles in the internal.

No matter how hard managers work, however, things happen. And when they do, an exile is bound to escape, flooding our awareness with its difficult emotions, causing firefighters to rush and calm us by any means necessary.

Let's return to Joannie as an example. After her divorce, she trudged into her women's Bible study just as an attendee was apprising the group on Joannie's ex-husband's social media post: "He looks blissfully smitten by the curvy new Mrs.!"

Heat climbed Joannie's face. Shame, jealousy, and rage prompted her to turn around and rush to her car. She sped out of the parking lot to buy three pints of cookies and cream—finishing them in one sitting.

Firefighter parts will try to distract us from pain using benign activities like sleeping, lulling us with entertainment, or—as in Joannie's case—compulsively eating ice cream. If these tactics fail to soothe us, they will up the ante and resort to more destructive acts. Cutting, getting intoxicated, driving recklessly, and suicide are examples of more dangerous firefighter activities.

EXAMPLE: ANNIKA'S GRIEF

Let's say Annika's teenage son overdosed on opioids. For the sake of simplicity, let's also pretend she only has three parts: one manager, one firefighter, and one exile.

Annika's tragic loss causes her exile to feel like the world's worst mom for failing to save him from fentanyl. Her firefighter part convinces her to drain a bottle of Chardonnay every night to avoid feeling her exile's guilt. Seeing this ritual, her inner critic (her manager part) responds by censuring her: *Shame on you for falling off the wagon after years of being sober!* The louder the critic gets, the more shame Annika's exile feels—which fuels her firefighter to drop even more wine bottles into her grocery cart.

For Annika, grieving wholeheartedly starts when she appreciates her protector parts, both manager and firefighter, as well as their positive intentions for her. Doing so will eventually help them relax, so Annika can befriend her exile, which in turn will help it expel its guilt and shame. Indeed, befriending our grieving parts (exiles) with relentless compassion will help them release their burden. This outcome—known as *unburdening*—is what we are after. Why? Because every time we unburden, we are also liberating more space within ourselves. And since our body is the temple of the Holy Spirit (1 Corinthians 6:19), the more we unburden, the more God's Spirit can occupy more of us.

IFS AND OTHER TECHNIQUES

Learning about IFS may be easier if you can connect it to something you are more familiar with, like contemplative prayer or inner healing ministry. In these spiritual formation exercises, spiritual directors lead directees through an imaginative experience of encountering Jesus. These established ways of relating to God within Christianity utilize similar dynamics as IFS—listening inwardly and trusting our imagination.

Another modality you may be aware of is the Enneagram, a way of understanding personality types, which some have traced back to ancient Egypt. Others claim there are hints of the Enneagram within Homer's classic work *The Odyssey*, while still others suggest the desert mothers and fathers, led by a fourth century mystic, Evagrius Ponticus, as its chief architects.[11]

The Enneagram offers "nine patterns of character structure archetypes . . . that shape how we think, feel, and act."[12] These types are Reformer, Helper, Achiever, Individualist, Investigator, Loyalist, Enthusiast, Challenger, and Peacemaker.[13] Entire books and courses exist to enlighten us on the complexities of this rich model. For our purposes, let's focus on the three intelligence centers, or the main way we perceive the world: our mind (rational thinking), heart (feeling and emotions), and body (instinctive or gut), as we bridge the Enneagram with IFS.

Let's peek into what Tammy Sollenberger, certified IFS therapist and host of The One Inside podcast, and Joan Ryan, an Enneagram expert, wrote regarding the two models. While they could not find a direct correlation of a specific part to a specific Enneagram type, Ryan and Sollenberger offered the following general observations:

The heart, or emotionally sensitive types, are Types 2, 3 and 4. The key parts we expect to find here are concerned with image, connection, and feelings. The underlying fuel or burden which we would expect to find in their exiles is grief.

The head, or mentally centered types, are Types 5, 6, and 7; they lead with their minds. They share high reliance on mental skills, analysis, and logic. The key parts we expect to find here are concerned with preparedness, predictability, and certainty. The underlying fuel or burden which we would expect to find in their exiles is fear.

The body-centered types include Types 8, 9 and 1; they lead with their gut or bodily instincts. The key parts we expect to find here are concerned with control, belonging, and being heard. The underlying fuel or burden which we would expect to find in exiles here is anger.[14]

Regardless of our Enneagram type, Ryan and Sollenberger believe we all have one common part: inner critics. These protectors may feel and sound different from type to type, but like it or not, critical parts live inside all of us.

DIPPING INSIDE

Congratulations on completing a chapter on a psychological model! You are one step closer to helping your entire internal system grieve. Let's transition from learning and switch to experiencing. (Pro tip: Consider bookmarking this section in case you need the refresher prior to checking in with your internal system in future chapters.)

Preparing to look inward. Attending to your body may help you shift your focus from the outside—such as where you are sitting down—to your inner world.

Tune into what your body needs. If you are sensing the need to stand up and stretch, do it. Rub tired muscles. Roll your shoulders. Inhale and expand your stomach, the marker for deep, diaphragmic breathing. Check in with your body and ask if it needs anything else. A snack? Beverage? Go ahead and meet your physical needs before settling back in. Please also grab a pen. You can write here as you go or choose to journal in a separate book, especially if you need more space.

When you are ready, switch your focus inward. Take your time as you go through each prompt. No need to think up anything; simply observe what happens internally.

Prompts for your parts. Engaging your parts with the following questions will reveal their presence. So, let's begin with asking if any parts has any observations or questions. Write down anything you sense.

_____

_____

_____

_____

Is there any feeling or sentiment about the prospect of using IFS to help you grieve? For instance, is there fear or dread? Doubt this could work? Excitement? Impatience?

_____

_____

_____

_____

Record any other reactions as well, including thoughts like *What's for dinner?* or a reminder of your extensive to-do list. (Tell these parts you will attend to their concerns at the right time, but not now.)

_____

_____

_____

_____

Scan your body from head to toe. Does a memory resurface just now? Does your chest feel tight? Is your heart racing? Write all the sensations you are detecting.

_____

_____

_____

_____

Look at the notes you have scribbled above. They represent *your* parts. So how about greeting them? Tell them something like "I hear you," "Glad you are here," or something along these lines.

Observe what happens when you show them attention. Do you sense relief inside? Perhaps you can breathe easier. Record everything you notice.

_____

_____

_____

_____

When you are ready to resume attending to the outside world again, thank the parts that showed up. Note any response from your internal system.

_____

_____

_____

_____

If you did not notice any sensations, keep an open heart. See if your parts drop in later tonight (like through dreams) or in the days to follow. Dick—likely the world's top authority on parts and their behavior, by virtue of his role as the theory's founder—has remarked that parts reward persistence and patience.[15] You can repeat what we just did and see if you notice any inward responses this time. Record your answers so you will have a way to track your parts.

_____

_____

_____

_____

3

IFS and Christian Faith

M Y S M I L I N G M U S C L E S must have missed the flight.

For the first two years after moving to America, my face hardly wore a happy look. It was the mid-1990s, the era of *Beverly Hills 90210*. But knowing that Brenda Walsh (my favorite!) also moved to California and enrolled in a college failed to taper the pain of my goodbyes. The high school graduate who left Jakarta for Los Angeles boarded the plane with a broken heart—for leaving family, friends, not to mention delicious food.

Moving plucked me out of my support system. Flying home was not viable—not when a one-way trip consumed twenty-plus hours, plus a pretty penny. Calling cost too much. There was no iPhone to send an email or WhatsApp to text with; my misery predated these technologies. Besides, the vast physical distance also meant when I was awake, my people were not. Their daytime was my evening and vice versa.

Snail mail was the only accessible way to communicate. But what an apt description! The old-fashioned route of paper, envelope, and stamps took somewhere around six weeks to reach my recipients. *If* they got the letter—never a guarantee—their response would have taken at least as long.

These factors piled on more and more loneliness until a desperate idea developed. On a Saturday evening during my first semester, I dialed a particular local number. The phone rang a few times before a recorded greeting kicked in. "Hello, you've reached the office of Dr. —"

Click.

I disconnected without leaving a message because the reason for my call had nothing to do with academics—it was only to hear a human voice.

I felt *that* lonely.

Some regions in the United States are more communal than others. I know that now. But back when I first assimilated to living here, clutching values formed in collectivistic Indonesia, LA's individualism felt like a testy greeting of *nobody cares about you.* These struggles forced me to reevaluate faith issues. I could no longer afford to treat spirituality as something I inherited from my mother's line.

A FAMILY LEGACY

My great-grandfather was the only child of his well-heeled father and late mother. Yet *his* father disinherited him and willed everything to his second wife instead. Enraged, my great-grandfather skipped town, became a sailor, and drank too much. The stage was set for an encounter so powerful that its impact would extend beyond his lifetime.

Meanwhile, a couple of missionaries from Seattle, Washington, had been braving the arduous trek to Indonesia. They arrived on the island where my great-grandfather lived just as he returned from his seafaring voyage. When he attended their revival meeting, the foreigners netted their first convert in the Ambon Island.

According to his only daughter, my grandmother, once my great-grandfather traded alcohol abuse for Almighty God, he immediately lost any appetite for the substance. He emerged as a lay preacher and raised his family in the ways of the Lord. This explains how my mother grew up as a faithful churchgoer, including while pregnant with me. Which also means I started attending church from my first home—her womb.

As childhood turned into adolescence, I kept going to church and reading my Bible, although my walk with Christ was largely orchestrated by my parents. Those desolate college days changed everything, though. I remember concluding, *Guess I'll have to find out if the God they told me about is real.*

Since then I have faced—and conquered—more episodes of loneliness. Losses. Heartbreaks, both personal and professional. So many disappointments, delays, distresses—plural all around. These trials pushed me to my knees, where I learned to exercise my spiritual muscles. I sought God for myself. Now, whenever something bothers me, I pray. Fast. Cry out to the God of my family. Dig into the Bible for fortification against these temporal challenges (2 Corinthians 4:18). Because God has defended me against every challenge, I can echo David's testimony: "No one who hopes in [God] will ever be put to shame" (Psalm 25:3). I have found Jesus to be the friend who sticks closer than any brother, sister, or relative (Proverbs 18:24).

It is this spiritual background I lean on to evaluate the compatibility of IFS with Christianity.

SPIRIT AND SOUL, SELF AND PARTS

The Bible's job is to describe God's loving plan for us. It is through the Bible we learn about Jesus' selfless task to save humanity from the fatal consequences of our own transgressions by sacrificing himself. This living document is not a psychology text.

Still, IFS concepts are present in the Bible, especially if you consider that what IFS calls Self, the Bible calls spirit.[1] In turn, the spirit contains Christlike qualities. Contrast Self characteristics with how the Bible describes our spirit and you will, indeed, find similarities. Take one of the 8 C's—*courage*—as an example. IFS says Self is courageous. Well, God did not give his children the spirit of fear (2 Timothy 1:7); therefore, our spirit *is* naturally courageous.

If Self is synonymous with spirit, parts are synonymous with soul. Or, the way I think about it, the parts we are referring to are parts of our soul. But what is spirit? And soul?

Your *spirit* is the channel you use to deal with *spiritual* issues. Because God is Spirit (John 4:24), he communicates to your spirit. Listen to the following explanation from Joseph Bayly, a father who wrote a book after burying three of his seven children: "A spirit is the real person, the part of us that nobody can see, the part that doesn't die. It's the inside you that says, 'God, I love you,' when you don't even move your lips; that makes you glad when you obey and unhappy when you don't."[2] In other words, if you have ever longed for the truth or drawn closer to your Maker, this desire likely stemmed from your spirit.

In contrast, your *soul* defines who you are as a unique person. Aspirations you yearn for, the hobbies you enjoy, who you associate with, the way you think, whether you default to cereal or coffee for breakfast, they are all driven by your soul. The late pastor Jack Hayford described the soul as the entity that "sits in the driver's seat. If it is dysfunctional in any way by reason of past habits, pains, or needed repairs, your whole being is affected. Just as broken walls hindered the definition and control of the city, so your saved but unrestored human soul hinders progress."[3]

The presence of both a spirit and soul (or Self and parts) within you explains how you can be attuned to your pastor's sermon while the back of your mind is vexing about the latest rift separating your adult sons. Chances are, the word of God is capturing your spirit's attention while a part of your soul is anxious about your boys.

BIBLICAL FOUNDATIONS

Does our soul consist of parts? Many in Christendom would respond with a resounding yes. They believe the soul consists of three parts: mind, will, and emotion.[4] But with the rise of IFS, perhaps more Christians will allow for multiplicity of the soul beyond this classic definition.

The Creator is fond of utilizing patterns in creation. The most basic example is how the triune God—Father, Son, Spirit—created humans to, likewise, exist in a tripartite form—spirit, soul, body (1 Thessalonians 5:23).[5] Both the Old and New Testaments understand humanity as consisting of multiple inner realities. But let's start our review with the former.

The King James Version's family of modern translations (such as the ESV, NASB, and NKJV) translate David's prayer in Psalm 86:11 as "unite my heart to fear Your name." It was also David who wrote the following: "Bless the LORD, O my soul, and all that is within me, bless his holy name!" (Psalm 103:1 ESV). Why would David ask God to unite his heart if there were not factions in it? Why refer to "all that is within" if his soul consisted of only one solitary section?

But my favorite supporting verse for multiplicity in the Old Testament comes from Isaiah 61:1: "The Spirit of the Sovereign Lord is on me, because the Lord has anointed me to proclaim good news to the poor. He has sent me to bind up the *brokenhearted*, to proclaim freedom for the captives and release from darkness for the prisoners" (italics added). The original Hebrew for "brokenhearted" is *shabar*, which means to break in pieces.[6] Since grief is the price we pay for love,[7] when our loved ones leave, it makes sense for that departure to shatter our hearts into smithereens. Maybe even some shards. These sharp fragments—parts of our soul that react to grief in cutting ways—need our help to facilitate their own grieving.

JESUS: HUMANS ARE NON-MONOLITHIC

Maybe it was just David whose heart needed unity. Who knows, maybe his egregious sins splintered his heart. Or maybe only a grieving heart disintegrates.

Does the New Testament support multiplicity of the soul for everyone? According to Jesus, yes. He quoted Deuteronomy 6:5 when stating the following to be the greatest commandment: "Love the Lord your God with all your heart and with all your soul and with all your mind. This is the first and greatest commandment" (Matthew 22:37-38). Or, according to Mark's Gospel, "Love the Lord your God with all your heart and with all your soul and with all your mind and with all your strength" (Mark 12:30).

Jesus could have condensed the commandment to a concise "Love the Lord your God." But by detailing our heart, soul, mind, and strength in his response, he lends support to the notion that we are non-unitary beings. His answer also highlights how the components that make up our being have the capacity to operate independently from each other—at least to a degree. It *is* possible to love the Lord with our strength but not necessarily our soul, or vice versa. Otherwise, why would God need to specify we are to love him with all our heart *and* mind *and* soul *and* strength?

Loving God with only some of our existence is not just possible, it is also rampant. Consider, for instance, a volunteer who never misses the chance to help out every time the church is open. Since serving zaps our energy, it is fair to conclude she loves God with all her strength. Then again, if she does so out of desperation—to coax God to heal her father's pneumonia—can she truly claim her service as proof she loves God with her whole heart?

By instructing us to love God with all our heart, mind, soul, and strength, Jesus supports the notion of all humans as non-monolithic beings.

PAUL AND PARTS: 1 CORINTHIANS 12

What about the apostle Paul? Did he say anything about parts? Let's study 1 Corinthians 12 for the answer. In this chapter, Paul compares the body of Christ to a human body to illustrate the need for every member of the body of Christ to honor each other, regardless of our spiritual gifts or positions. We are to serve one another for the benefit of the whole, just like all parts of our body work together for our good.

Paul's analogy works because, obviously, the body consists of many parts. But what if we were to read his words with the principles of IFS in mind? Here is how 1 Corinthians 12:14 reads: "The body is not made up of one part but of many." The message still rings true if we apply verse 14 to the soul: "The soul is not made up of one part but of many."

In a similar fashion, while the rest of 1 Corinthians 12 clearly refers to the body, we can apply the message to our soul and its parts:

> The eye cannot say to the hand, "I don't need you!" And the head cannot say to the feet, "I don't need you!" On the contrary, those parts of the body that seem to be weaker are indispensable, and the parts that we think are less honorable we treat with special honor. And the parts that are unpresentable are treated with special modesty, while our presentable parts need no special treatment. But God has put the body together, giving greater honor to the parts that

lacked it, so that there should be no division in the body, but that its parts should have equal concern for each other. If one part suffers, every part suffers with it; if one part is honored, every part rejoices with it. (1 Corinthians 12:21-26)

All parts of our soul are interconnected. Managers, firefighters, and exiles need each other, the same way our eyes and head need the rest of the body. Vulnerable parts like exiles are treated with special care, in that protector parts spend their energy, day and night, to protect them. (Dick Schwartz wrote that some manager parts never sleep; their round-the-clock shift is intended to keep exiles from being triggered by the world around us.[8]) This is why, when something hurts or shames us (such as when our exiles are triggered), we sense an instinctive desire to retaliate, defend ourselves, self-soothe—the handiwork of our firefighters.

GRIEVING IN LIGHT OF 1 CORINTHIANS 12

Within 1 Corinthians 12 are invaluable insights for us as mourners. Let's highlight a few verses at a time to mine these gems and see how they might apply to our grieving parts.

♥ ♥ ♥

The eye cannot say to the hand, "I don't need you!" And the head cannot say to the feet, "I don't need you!" (v. 21)

Paul pinpointed the eye and the head as not having the right to reject other body parts. Why pick these two? Perhaps because of their importance. In Matthew 6:22, Jesus revealed the eye as the lamp of the body: "If your eyes are healthy, your whole body will be full of light." Whether the rest of the body lives in darkness or light hinges on the health of the eye. Such a vital role!

Spiritually speaking, Jesus is the head of the church (Ephesians 1:22-23). Practically speaking, nobody can remain alive without their head, while many have continued living without their feet.

Paul highlighted these vital body parts—the eye and the head— to drive home the point that they cannot dismiss other parts that appear less necessary, like hands or feet. Translated into our context, it means there are no parts of the soul (like protectors) that can dismiss grieving parts. We cannot ignore their grief either.

💙 💙 💙

On the contrary, those parts of the body that seem to be weaker are indispensable, and the parts that we think are less honorable we treat with special honor. (vv. 22-23)

We can read this section as a way to recognize how parts of the soul that managers and firefighters think are weaker and less honorable (like exiles) are indispensable and need to be treated with honor. This special treatment includes applying an extra dose of tenderness to exiles. For instance, when exiles show up in my work, I negotiate with any other parts that might impinge on them as these exiles attempt to share their burdens with my clients. I politely insist for other parts to give them a wide berth. Once exiles are unburdened, they typically return to their cheerful and carefree nature, the way they were before life burdened them down. These childlike parts are precious and truly indispensable.

💙 💙 💙

And the parts that are unpresentable are treated with special modesty, while our presentable parts need no special treatment. (vv. 23-24)

We could apply these verses to our soul by making sure that parts that are unpresentable (such as exiles) are treated with extra protection; our presentable parts (such as protectors) need no special treatment. Indeed, protector parts are resilient. Managers strategize to keep us safe while firefighters serve as our first line of defense against an attack, both perceived and real. Both groups of protectors interface with the world—unlike exiles, who are usually kept hidden.

❦ ❦ ❦

But God has put the body together, giving greater honor to the parts that lacked it, so that there should be no division in the body, but that its parts should have equal concern for each other. If one part suffers, every part suffers with it; if one part is honored, every part rejoices with it. (vv. 24-26)

What these verses say about the body are applicable to the soul. God has put the soul together so that it should have no division. Here is how *The Message* paraphrased the tail end of these verses: "If one part hurts, every other part is involved in the hurt, *and in the healing*. If one part flourishes, every other part enters into the exuberance" (italics added).

Our soul operates as a system. If one part is grieving, it will affect all the other parts—even if they do not give the appearance of mourning. But when parts that are weighed down with grief are willing to unburden, the relief will permeate the rest of the inner world, freeing protector parts from having to distance us from our grief.

DIPPING INSIDE

Review the section on preparing to look inward in chapter two if necessary.

When you are ready, ask your internal system, *How does this chapter land with you?* Take note of all the answers you sense.

_____

_____

_____

Is there a part that feels hesitant to move forward? Ask it to reveal its presence. Once you establish a connection with the part, remain curious and ask this part to share its misgivings. Jot them down.

_____

_____

_____

_____

Ask your part, along with any member of the Trinity, to review 1 Corinthians 12 with you. Discuss any objections your part might have about reading the text using an IFS lens. And since God— the divine Author of the passage—is also with you, please address any questions that emerge from your reading directly to him.

_____

_____

_____

_____

Next, ask the Lord to reveal what he thinks about IFS. What does God say about using the model to help you grieve? Write down his answers, including any verse(s) he may mention.

_____

_____

_____

_____

If you decide to grieve using IFS, what does the hesitant part need from you so it can relax its guard? Let the part know if you can fulfill its request.

_____

_____

_____

_____

Is there anything else the part wishes to tell you? Jot it down.

_____

_____

_____

_____

Before closing your internal session with this part, please thank it. With its permission, let's turn a corner and find the land where your protectors reside.

PART 2

Protectors

4

Plenty of Permission

LOLLI AND POPS' VIBRANT DECOR dragged my gaze to their gummies. *Papa enjoyed the sour ones.* See's Candies would have handed him a free truffle had he moseyed in. *And he always made a point to enter their store.* The oversized chairs in front of Macy's—where he and Mama would pause their shopping to people-watch—stood vacant, as though reserving their cushy seats for him.

These sights magnified my melancholy.

They don't know you're forever gone, Papa.

He loved this mall. Maybe that was why, only a year after he passed, I meandered here. But it did not take long for tears to form, ready to freefall off my face. My grieving parts were unprepared for this outing.

Nope. I shook my head. *Sobbing at the mall won't do.*

I scuttled away from Macy's and as I turned, a clothing store's window display snagged my attention. Under a "30% off sale!" announcement, two words in burnished copper summed up my world post-Papa: "Unexpected Directions."

Even though their marketing team meant it in an optimistic sense, I took the phrase as anything but. "Unexpected" described my father's death to a tee. He exercised multiple times a week, hours at a time. Barely carried any body fat. Won sports tournaments. One weekend he swam non-stop at our neighborhood gym, for hours, eventually breaking the local record.

Yet a heart attack felled this athletic man. How could this be?

Death snatched my father so stealthily that I shuttered my private practice, left the counseling center I directed, booked the earliest available flight, and moved in with my mom. But our joint forces felt feeble against the twin barrage of shock and sorrow.

Concentrating on anything longer than a Scripture verse was impossible for the first fuzzy weeks. My mind morphed into a sieve with oversized holes, draining any information I fed into it. Whether conversations or condolences, the words went by in a blur. I ended up spending a month and a half in my hometown, consoling my mother, helping her with practical tasks. Then I flew back to the United States.

Which was when I discovered how closely my office mirrored my heart. Deserted.

The consequence of closing my practice hit me then. Because I could not have anticipated how long my leave of absence was going to last, my clients fled to other providers. While this was understandable, the bitter reality of having no father *and* no income meant I had to rebuild my business from scratch.

Unexpected directions indeed.

FRESH GRIEF

When my grief was fresh, I lacked the ability to sit with my parts. They took turns blending with me almost all the time. I had no mental resources to distinguish one part from another, much less listen to what they all needed. It took a while for shock to slowly morph into resigned acceptance. It took even longer before the upheaval in our family settled into a new normal that was—is—somewhat tolerable.

If your loss has just happened, give yourself permission *not* to dive into the rest of this book right away. The early days following our losses are notoriously difficult. You may feel numb. Or the opposite, in that you have to claw your way out of a cacophony of different feelings and thoughts. When your grief is raw, count it an accomplishment if you can do simple self-care activities like getting up, showering, or brewing coffee. Working with your parts can wait until after you have seized some stability in this new reality.

Eventually, grief will loosen its grip on your windpipe. The mention of your beloved won't always choke you up. You will recover enough emotional bandwidth to grieve, giving you a wee bit more space to care for the grieving parts of your soul. Discerning what your internal world needs can wait until then.

Until when, exactly?

The answer will reveal itself to you as time goes on. But don't pin your hopes on resolving your grief after a certain amount of time, like a year.[1] Yes, you can use this major milestone to measure how you and your parts are faring. Are you sleeping better? How are you with places that remind you of your loss, like me and the mall? Commemorating the first anniversary of your loss by holding a family gathering, for instance, can minister a measure of healing. At the same time, it is natural to still grapple with grief long after the first anniversary.

Give your parts the liberty to grieve at their own pace.

PROTECTORS' PERMISSION

Author and theologian Jerry Sittser lost his wife, daughter, and mother when a speeding car jumped its lane and smashed into

the van Sittser was driving. Reflecting on his losses and the resulting burden—having to mourn the death of multiple family
members while simultaneously parenting the rest of his children
alone—caused Sittser to remark, "Busyness and exhaustion can
sabotage healing."[2]

His observation rings true. If it were up to them, protector
parts would do *anything* to distance us from our messy feelings.
We will discuss their fears in the next three chapters, but for now,
see if you recognize thoughts like these: *Who wants to wail so hard
your whole body is shaking? Who would relish the low brought about
by despair and sorrow? Who would choose to live disoriented and
hopeless? Nobody! So stop focusing on the past. What's gone is gone.*

If thoughts like these have crossed your mind, chances are, you
have heard from some of your protectors.

EDUCATING PROTECTORS

Our protective system—comprised of parts whose jobs are to
protect us from emotional flooding, like crying nonstop, isolating
ourselves, having no appetite—appreciates relevant facts and
truths it may not have known before. For instance, protectors
often soften when they realize things are better now, compared
to childhood.

So here comes a question for your protectors: What if there is
a way for you to grieve without having to shut down the entire
system? Yes, it will still be painful to recall the life you used to
have. But no, the process does not have to paralyze you.

If IFS can help you grieve in a safe manner, would your protectors let you do it?

One reason grief is undesirable is the overwhelming soup
of feelings it stirs up. Dr. Kenneth Doka, a prolific author and
speaker on the subject of grief, explains it this way: "We rarely experience one dominant emotion at a time. We can feel depression,

anger, disbelief all at once. We are a hive of emotions."[3] If his assessment feels intimidating, take a deep breath. IFS can help you tease apart one emotion from the next.

How? We can identify parts based on how they manifest, including the beliefs, thoughts, or feelings they hold. Different parts care about different things. So if you are in the midst of connecting with a sad part and feel a wave of fear, ask the sad part if the fear belongs to it. If the answer is yes, continue working with that part. But if the answer is no, then another part is feeling afraid, and you are sensing this newcomer's fear. Acknowledge the new part and ask for space so you can continue working with the sad part.

Here is an example: Jesse, a 31-year-old man, runs an independent coffee shop with his business partner, Matt. Following news that Matt's dad had died, Jesse dreamed of his grandmother several nights in a row. She died when he was only 7; but in his vivid dreams, even though Granny had died, by some miracle she lived again. Jesse woke up from these dreams deeply sad.

I asked Jesse to focus internally to get in touch with his internal system. "Ask your parts, who wants to speak first?"

(The answer to this question emerges when you attend to what is happening inside. For instance, if there is a persistent thought, it could come from a part who desperately needs your attention. You may also register a physical sensation, feel an emotion, see a scene, or have a memory flashback.)

Jesse closed his eyes and remained silent. Moments later he reported, "I had this thought: *Matt doesn't talk about his dad. He didn't even cry at the funeral. So why am I still moping about Granny's death?*"

(When Jesse listened to his inner system, one part piped up with the thought he then shared with me.)

I asked Jesse how he felt toward the part that shared its opinion.

"I can understand where it's coming from," he answered. "Matt's loss is fresh while mine is ancient, so it makes sense for the part to think I shouldn't be sad over my loss."

"Would you share your understanding with this part?"

Once he signaled he had done so, I asked again. "What are you noticing now?"

"This thought came to me: *It's only your grandma who died. Big deal. It wasn't like you lost a parent.*"

"Did this thought come from the same part you talked to before? Just ask it."

(If you are unsure about a turn of events, you can always ask the last part you connected with if it had something to do with the development.)

After checking inside, Jesse confirmed, "No, it wasn't."

"Let's find out from the first part if it has told you everything. If it says yes and it doesn't mind you shifting your focus, we'll talk to the second part."

Another period of silence ensued as Jesse conferred with his system. Then he responded, "The first part is fine."

"Okay, let's focus on the second part. How do you notice it?"

"It's reminding me how every group I was affiliated with ignored Granny's death. My friends acted like it didn't happen. Nobody asked me about it at church. My mom told me to stop crying. She said, 'Granny wasn't even your biological grandmother! She married Gramps after your biological grandmother died. So why are you so torn up?'"

"Jesse, does it seem this part wants to keep you from grieving Granny's death?"

He nodded. "The part quoted what my mom's friends said at the funeral. 'You're lucky you only lost a grandparent. That's not as bad as losing a parent.' This part is making it hard for me to feel sad over Granny's death."

The point of Jesse's story is to show you an example of discerning one part from another. This ability—what IFS often calls a "parts detector"—will continue to grow if you continue working with your parts.

We will return to his story a bit later.

HALF PERMISSIONS

Your parts carry varied levels of grief: how closely the parts interacted with the person (or pet or aspiration) you lost, the parts' psychological age, and their function in your internal system can all determine how affected they are by the loss you incurred.

In addition, some parts—namely, protectors—may be hesitant to let you access your grief, for reasons we will delve into in the next few chapters. Do not proceed until you have negotiated with all the parts that may object to letting you grieve. That is, please do not steamroll ahead if you feel some form of internal opposition, including hesitancy or uneasiness. If you move forward anyway, you risk displeasing the opposing part, which may then devise a backlash. Instead of sidestepping the reluctant part, therefore, listen to its concerns.

Here is Nora's story to illustrate. The 53-year-old woman divorced Hector years ago because he was an angry drunk. After guzzling beer like his life depended on it, he would hit her. Once sobriety returned, dragging with it awareness of the bruises on Nora's face, he would profusely apologize—but the cycle continued anyway.

They had both remarried to different spouses when Nora heard that Hector's kidneys finally failed. His demise left Nora with mixed feelings. She was mindful of sadness, but from far away. Curious, Nora asked inside, *Is there a part restraining me from fully feeling sad?* The answer she sensed confirmed her suspicion. One part insisted, *It's not your place to grieve; Hector isn't yours anymore.*

Nora thanked this part for its feedback. She then explained to the part how anyone who was affected by Hector's death was welcome to mourn. Grieving was a normal reaction to loss, regardless of status. Therefore, it was fine for her to grieve Hector even though he was her ex.

The protector listened to Nora's explanation. It only relented, however, when she promised to inform her husband about Hector's death. The part promised to stand down if her husband let Nora mourn.

Nora benefited twice from this internal negotiation. First, getting her husband's blessing to grieve Hector's death paved the way to mourn her ex without fearing she was somehow violating her husband's trust. Second, Nora also learned more about this particular protector. Its initial insistence in keeping her from grieving Hector's death was driven by its protectiveness of her current marriage. This part wanted to keep Nora's husband from being jealous and leave her. Its intention was to protect Nora from getting divorced again.

PROTECTORS ARE THE BOSS

Dick Schwartz often tells protectors, "You are the boss." By this he means protectors have the power to decide whether and when to make internal space for us.

We see this example when Nora respected the part that initially objected to let her grieve Hector's death. She took the time to negotiate with this part until it relented. It was only after this protector gave her the access that she felt the freedom to remember the sweet times she shared with sober Hector. This led her to shed a few tears over the irony of him dying after succeeding to kick his addiction.

Keep Dick's line handy whenever you negotiate with protectors.

DIPPING INSIDE

How are you doing as we conclude this chapter? Ask inside. Do any of your protectors have any comments? For instance, if you sense a reluctance to cry or to recall the loss you experienced, that thought or impulse likely came from a protector. Jot everything you notice internally here.

_____

_____

_____

_____

Remind your protectors they are the boss: they can tell you when to proceed and when to pause as you work with your more vulnerable parts. Let them know you can learn to distinguish one part from the next, focusing on one part at a time, so you won't end up with a smorgasbord of difficult emotions at once.

How do your protectors react at this announcement? Write down what you are noticing. This may include direct answers, relief, or perhaps more peace.

_____

_____

_____

_____

Is there any protector whose concern we have not covered? If so, jot it down.

_____

_____

If you have an answer for this part, share it with your part directly. You can also ask this part to wait in case its concern is covered in the next couple chapters.

Finally, please appreciate all of the parts who showed up in this session.

John, Audrey, the Wreathed Hornbill bird, Mama, and Papa (Bali, Indonesia). Just as the bird wouldn't have perched on my arm without my permission, you can't approach your exiles without your protectors' permission.

Two Common Managers

THINKERS AND CRITICS

DUELING NARRATIVES SHADOWED Jesus of Nazareth from birth to death. Is he God—or the average Joe, Jewish edition?

Let's take Philip. This disciple referred to Jesus as "the son of Joseph" (John 1:43-45). Since Joseph married Jesus' mother, the designation makes sense. Except an unprecedented incident interrupted their wedding plans.

"Joseph, I'm pregnant. But it happened supernaturally. No, really!" Mary blurted out.

Given this news, the groom-to-be believed it was best for them to separate. But then an angel appeared. The supernatural being verified Mary's story before instructing Joseph to give the baby the name Jesus (Matthew 1:18-25).

Imagine the impact of this tale on their neighbors. Can you picture the Nazareth townsfolk nodding their heads, smiling their acceptance? Me neither. A more likely scenario would have involved some sneering. "We *know* how that baby got into Mary's belly, alright. Angelic visitations my foot!"

Another competing chronicle shrouded Jesus' crucifixion. On the one hand was the slew of prophecies, some by Jesus himself, promising a resurrection three days following his execution. On the other, the guards—posted by the tomb to insure nobody could steal his corpse—spread stories about how Jesus' disciples went behind their backs and did it anyway (Matthew 28:13-15). Which was it? Is Jesus the promised Messiah or a mere wannabe? It is up to each seeker to decide.

There are many resources to aid our faith journey, including *The Chosen*, a multiseason television show on the life of Jesus from the perspective of eyewitnesses. More than providing mere entertainment, *The Chosen* has drawn many, including atheists, to "binge Jesus"—one of the show's catchphrases.[1] But if you asked a thinking part about whether Jesus was a truth-teller or slick cult leader, you would likely get a response like *let's use something more substantial than entertainment*. Thinking parts prefer to examine the issue by researching the veracity of the Bible or studying thick theological tomes and commentaries—maybe books by apologists.

That is because thinking parts, as their name implies, employ thinking and analyzing as a way of life.

THINKING PARTS

Everyone has them. Society rewards those with a strong tendency to engage them. They are some of the most common manager parts.

I am referring to "thinking parts"—the ones that assist us in many of life's most crucial tasks. For instance, if you have ever aced an exam, won a scholarship, profited in the stock market, avoided being scammed, or made ends meet, you have these parts to thank.

Like all manager parts, thinking parts aim to keep us safe. They do so by controlling both our external and internal environment;

exerting control in the internal world involves the use of logic to scrub feelings from our awareness. No feelings means no messy emotional reaction, which is what thinking parts prefer.

Have you heard any of these sentiments, whether in your own head or spoken by someone else?

- *There's no need to grieve. Death is a part of life.*
- *Crying won't undo your loss.*
- *Why are you this upset?* [Insert the logic next, such as] *You two weren't even close toward the end; it's only a pet; you knew the end was near.*
- *Throwing a pity party won't pay the bills. Get up and get to work.*
- *Cheer up! Your loved one is now pain-free.*

I borrowed the last example from a friend. Like me, Olivia had to bury a parent. Unlike me, however, her grieving journey was prolonged. She had to watch her mother fight ovarian cancer for eight miserable months. One day she and I met, swapping stories in search of a slice of comfort. Ignoring her cappuccino, Olivia's voice cracked when she shared how, following her mother's death, a fellow choir member advised her, "Cheer up! Your mom isn't in pain anymore."

Maybe you have experienced what Olivia encountered—an insensitive response in the face of your sorrow. Thinking parts can seem callous when faced with deep suffering. According to Dick Schwartz, thinking parts "may be highly intellectual and effective at problem solving, but also obsessed with pushing feelings away."[2] Indeed, thinking parts strive to steer us clear of painful emotions like sadness and sorrow, including memories that can trigger them, to keep our internal systems from being overwhelmed.

But why do thinking parts dread this state? For two reasons. First, when negative emotions overwhelm us, this flood of feelings can keep us from functioning, be it in caring for our little kids or performing at work. Maybe you have heard stories of mourners who were paralyzed from moving onward in life due to a grievous loss.

When this paralysis happens, firefighter parts—which we will meet in chapter seven—swoop in with their audacious attempts to soothe us. This is the second reason managers, including thinking parts, prefer to sanitize our inner worlds from difficult feelings. Managers fear firefighters' dangerous reactivity. Indeed, because everything is fair game to firefighters, they give no flip to caution or common sense. They will entice us with dangerous behavior if need be—drinking, drug use, binge eating, reckless driving, or even suicide—if it means eliminating our emotional pain.

This is why thinking parts try to minimize wailing, trembling, and any other expressive display of negative emotions associated with grieving. They strive to stifle our vulnerable parts from overtaking us with their swollen emotions.

But there is one tiny problem with this strategy.

It does not work.

Just ask Dr. Marc Brackett, the founding director of the Yale Center for Emotional Intelligence. He explains, "When we ignore our feelings, or suppress them, they only become stronger."[3] By suppressing our exiled parts, thinking parts (and other managers) are also creating a built-in irony; preventing us from getting in touch with grief may lead to complicated mourning.[4]

Thankfully, it is possible to feel without being swept away by a tornado of feelings. Dick Schwartz discovered the key when he started working with his clients' parts. We can prevent an emotional cascade by asking parts—including exiles—not to overwhelm us with their feelings.[5]

INTERNAL VERSUS EXTERNAL CRYING

Here is another piece of information that thinking parts might appreciate: just because parts have an emotional reaction on the inside does not mean we will also experience that same reaction.

I have sat with many clients who modeled this phenomenon. For instance, in her mind's eye, Susan saw a terrified little part crying and curled up in the fetal position. Despite the onslaught of her part's fear, Susan showed no agitation. Her loving and steady presence eventually calmed the part. Pete—who has clearly spent loads of time at the gym—was negotiating with an irritated part when, in his mind's eye, the part slammed its fist on the wall. I am thankful Pete maintained his composure throughout the entire ordeal. He could have easily punched a hole in my office if he had mimicked his part's reaction physically.

How can parts feel something on the inside that we do not always feel ourselves? It has to do with the amount of blending. Since blending happens on a spectrum, when we are only slightly blended with a part, that part's emotion does not overtake us.

THINKING PARTS GRIEVE TOO

Don't let the above discussion mislead you into believing thinking parts are exempted from grief. They are not. But rather than *feeling* their grief, they resort to—surprise!—*thinking* it. Here is an example from C. S. Lewis, one of the most famous thinkers in Christianity. Lewis was the creative genius behind the Chronicles of Narnia and *The Screwtape Letters*. In addition, he also wrote apologetics such as *Mere Christianity*, *Miracles*, and *the Problem of Pain*—and, after his wife's death, *A Grief Observed*. Notice his nod to his thinking part: "I not only live each endless day in grief, but live each day thinking about living each day in grief."[6]

If you, like Lewis, have a strong thinking part, this might mean you think about the deceased (or the circumstances surrounding your loss) an awful lot. It might also mean you may not emote much about it, preferring to channel your grief into doing something productive instead.

Ken Doka, who has written and taught extensively on grief, coined four categories of grievers. He based them on whether the mourners express grief primarily through emoting or thinking: heart grievers, head grievers, heart + head grievers, and heart vs. head grievers.[7]

Heart grievers possess, and express, strong feelings of grief. In contrast, heart + head grievers toggle back and forth between the two reactions to grief. What Doka calls heart v. head grievers, however, sound like mourners whose protector parts prevent them from accessing exiled parts that carry difficult feelings surrounding grief.

Let's zero in on head grievers. If you, like these mourners, deal with your losses primarily through your intellect (that is, by relying on your thinking parts), take note of Doka's observation: "Many of the most initially troubling aspects of grief involve impaired cognitive activity. Confusion, disorientation, an inability to concentrate, and disorganized thought may be difficult issues for head grievers."[8] Forgetfulness and memory loss are two additional symptoms.

The loss of mental acuity would scare anyone. But if you are used to functioning mostly from your head, this list of symptoms must sound alarm bells inside. Suffice it to say, thinking parts grieve too.

INNER CRITICS

You can spot inner critics by—you guessed it—their critical tone. If you have heard the following (or something similar) within you, you have likely heard from your critic:

- *Look at you, glued to TikTok like some middle schooler! Don't you have anything better to do?*

- *Stop that sniveling! Crying is for weaklings.*
- *What a special kind of loser you are, groveling after a spouse who was never there for you to begin with.*
- *You think Ma would approve of you*—insert a self-medicating behavior, like eating, drinking, maxing out your credit card, etc.—*just because she's passed on?*

These manager parts do their work by criticizing us. This much is self-evident. What can be more counterintuitive is the purpose behind their work; like misled parents who believe they can shame their kids into behaving better, our critical parts assail us because they mean well.

With enough criticism, we will drop all desires to try—which will then protect us from failing. Also, by judging us first, these parts hope they will improve our conduct and keep others from having to criticize us (which will potentially hurt more). In the absence of community and mentors, inner critics step in to serve as our inner guru.[9]

The last category was something Roy experienced. His father died in a freak accident when he was only eleven. The boy emulated Dad in every way, so when he died, Roy lost his mentor. Seeing this, a critical part began to chide Roy at every turn, with the expressed purpose to toughen him up against life's difficulties. But when Roy informed the part he is now an adult, the part remained unfazed. As Roy continued to befriend this part, he discovered the part was 82 years old—decades older than Roy. (The critical part might have claimed it was older so it can assert its right to continue doing its job and whip Roy into shape, emotionally speaking.)

Critics will not relent until they know the exiles they have been protecting—like the eleven-year-old, fatherless boy—can survive this cruel world. They work hard for this very reason. But they are often clueless that their way of helping is also creating a bind.

This is what I mean: critics' work consists of hurtful attacks, with firefighters being their main target. Critics consider firefighters reckless rascals with no regard for safety. But firefighters are thick-skinned. They give no heed to societal norms, much less inner critics' chastisement. No amount of Scripture-shaming or plain old criticisms will weaken their resolve.

Meanwhile, the harshness from inner critics is generating shame that is circulating on the inside. Who do you think will digest it? Our most vulnerable parts. Often, it is our exiles that wind up absorbing our shame and guilt: *I must be an impostor. A real Christian wouldn't be this devastated just because of a loss.*

But when our exiles feel ashamed, firefighters will again rush to their rescue—because wherever there is injury, firefighters will strive to dull the pain.[10] This feedback loop will continue unless you and I step in and befriend the parts involved, which is what we will do next.

DIPPING INSIDE

Parts are like pets—both appreciate time with us. So how about greeting the parts in your system whose job has to do with thinking? Aim your greeting to where you sense their presence (chances are, it is in or around your head). How do you feel toward your thinking part(s)? If the answer is any of the 8 C's, let them feel your sentiment, coming from your heart.

Notice how your thinking part responds. This response can take the form of thoughts, pictures, sensations, or memories. Please acknowledge its response in your own way.

_____

_____

_____

_____

Ask your part how it is doing with the loss you are mourning. Is there any concern about increased confusion, disorientation, inability to concentrate, disorganized thought, or memory impairment since you suffered this loss? Jot the answer here.

What does your part need from you to help with these symptoms? For instance, it might want you to seek medical attention if these cognitive disturbances persist.

Ask inside, *Is there anything I can do to help ease your grief?* If you can fulfill its request, let it know.

Thinking parts, as smart as they are, cannot fill the gaping void due to our loss. We cannot solve emotional needs using rational means. As an insightful client once observed, "No amount of competence can compensate for emotional needs."

Feel free to use the above quote with your own thinking part. Listen to any feedback it might give you and then ask, *Are you willing to step back when it's time for me to help my exiles with their grief?*

If the answer is some permutation of no, remind your thinking part we can ask exiles not to overwhelm. See if this makes any difference. If not, ask what needs to happen before your thinking part can relent. Circle back to the part once you have met the condition it placed.

Now, let's turn our attention to your critics. Review the section on inner critics and the bullet points of examples. Did you resonate with any? A yes reveals the presence of your own critic. If so, focus on where you sense the critic's headquarters to be, in or around your body. Are you curious as to why it would treat you harshly while you are grieving? If so, convey this question to your critic and wait for its response.

_____

_____

If you sense pushback, affirm how you are here to understand—
not judge—it. See if this helps relax your critic. If not, you could
be blended with parts that dislike your critic. Like people, parts
don't like to be criticized, so critics are wildly unpopular in the
internal world.

Let the parts that shun your critics know—*If you relax, I can
help my critic be kinder.*

Once you feel these other parts relent, thank them. Then, ask
your critic if there is anything it would like you to know about
itself or its job. Jot down what it says.

_____

_____

_____

_____

Ask it this question: *What are you afraid will happen if you don't
berate me or the way I grieve?* Jot down its answer.

_____

_____

_____

_____

If it gives you some kind of positive intention as the reason
behind its inaudible tongue-lashing, inform it of Proverbs 19:20,
"Listen to advice and accept discipline, and at the end you will
be counted among the wise." This verse explains the way to get

wisdom is by listening to advice and instruction—*not* criticism. How is your critic doing in light of this verse?

_____

_____

_____

_____

Please also let your part know that by criticizing you, it is adding to your burden. Check with your part how it feels about this news.

_____

_____

_____

_____

Let your critic know this book will inform you on how to alleviate your exiles from their grief. If the part has a response, write it down.

_____

_____

_____

_____

Now, ask your critic about its job satisfaction: *Does criticizing me bring you satisfaction? Or do you get wearied by your job? How do the other parts relate to you?*

_____

_____

Just about every critic I have interviewed admitted some form of dissatisfaction with its job, while feeling obligated to keep going (for the sake of the person they were protecting). If your critic expresses a similar response, please remind it of Jesus' offer in Matthew 11:28-30: "Come to me, all you who are weary and burdened, and I will give you rest. Take my yoke upon you and learn from me, for I am gentle and humble in heart, and you will find rest for your souls. For my yoke is easy and my burden is light." Is your critic willing to learn from Jesus? He, too, wants you protected—but his ways are gentle and light.

If your critic is hesitant to commit, don't force it. Ask it to explain its reluctance. Maybe you can introduce the gentle Savior to your part. Let it know how Jesus doesn't shame anybody. He won't shame the critic for criticizing you either. But if your part says yes, set an intention to spend more time with both Jesus and your critical part. Ask the Lord to show you and your part how he motivates you. Write what you sense Jesus is saying to you here.

Please thank the Lord and all your parts once you are ready to end this session with your inner world.

6

Your Most Religious Part

IMAGINE SETTLING INTO a luxurious corner office at the start of a new workweek. Just one of the perks of running a multimillion-dollar empire—the prize-winning interior designer you hired to style the room has done a meticulous, and fabulous, job.

Propped by a plush leather chair, your eyes scan the spreadsheet. The plump numbers it reports spread your face into a satisfied smile. *These latest figures are amazing.* Another profitable year for the chain of jewelry stores you built. Despite the dismal economy, these shops—in major metropolitan areas across five states—have performed beyond expectations.

Two raps on the door intrude into your reverie.

"I, uh, I am sorry for interrupting," your executive assistant rushes in, phone in hand, speaking a million miles a minute. "Troy called. A flash mob ransacked our store in California and stole half a million dollars' worth of jewelry. As I pressed for details, Ryan texted. The same happened in Dallas. And then Mario in Atlanta—"

Footsteps rush forward. Your secretary, harried-looking, blurts, "A hurricane destroyed your mansion. Only the butler managed to escape."

Yet another agitated assistant jostles in. He exclaims, "I have a state trooper on the phone. A semi-trailer jackknifed your kids' car and they died upon impact."

This is too much!

"Stop!" you yell. Standing up, you usher everyone out despite their protests. You close the door to reclaim some peace. But blood rushes to your head, leaving your insides feeling like someone left the blender on the fastest setting. Bits of thoughts, feelings, and sensations are clashing with each other.

You dial your spouse, your safe zone. Facing this nightmare together will help, right?

But when you recap the string of horrible news, yet another shock greets you. "Just roll over and die," your spouse sneers.

Now imagine that days after these disasters, your small group drops in for a visit—the same group of Christians you've prayed and celebrated praise reports with for years.

Yet after a respectful silence, one person pipes up with, "These calamities happened to you because you sinned."

Another has the gall to blame your kids as culprits: "I'm sure they backslid. Their sin must've killed them."

A STORY WORTH READING

If the narrative seems familiar, let me admit: I pulled a real-life story from the Bible and fictionalized it. An avalanche of tragedies befell a historical figure named Job, "the richest person in that entire area" (Job 1:3 NLT). He had amassed an enviable number of herds and hired a cadre of staff. But within the first two chapters in the book bearing his name, Job lost of all of the above—and his health—in short succession.

Never one to act mushy, Mrs. Job advised Job to kill himself (Job 2:1-9). Makes me wonder if she married him for his moolah. Her motivation aside, there are a couple of reasons I featured

Job's story here. First, to whet your appetite. The book of Job—in the middle of the Old Testament—is worthy of your time. Job suffered from multiple violent losses, leaving him stunned at best and traumatized at worst. If he lived today, experts would have labeled Job's grief as complicated. Learning how an actual man bounced back from an untold amount of agony can inspire you to arise from your own ashes of grief.

I also fictionalized his story to highlight the religious parts in the narrative. It is easy to miss the significance of Job's account if you have heard it before. Yet his saga illustrates how seamlessly parts take over our mouths and mental faculties to express themselves.

INTRODUCING RELIGIOUS PARTS

Behold religious parts.

Think of them as a specialized subset of thinking parts, the ones we met in the last chapter. They function like ordinary thinking parts, in that both employ logic to support their position. But religious parts come alive around spiritual and religious matters; hence their name.

My guess is religious parts exist in every person who holds a spiritual or religious belief system. But because I am not sufficiently trained in other religions to substantiate an expert opinion, let me restrict my observations to Christian circles alone. The Christians you interact with—including those who used to identify as such, but not anymore—likely carry their own religious parts, even if these parts may not always operate in the forefront of their awareness.

We can also detect religious parts within the Bible. For instance, Job's three friends visited him with their religious parts tagging along, getting progressively more blended with them as things intensified.

But that brings up a question. How can you tell if you are talking to a religious part?

IDENTIFYING RELIGIOUS PARTS

Insensitivity. How do you respond to a suicidal friend? I hope it's with a hearty dose of compassion. But if religious parts lead the way, you will likely get anything but. For instance, after Job disclosed his death wish (Job 6:8-9), his friend Bildad argued, "Does God subvert judgment? Or does the Almighty pervert justice? If your sons have sinned against him, he has cast them away for their transgression" (Job 8:3-4 NKJV).

Translation: *God killed your sons because they were sinning, Job.*

We know Bildad's religious part formulated his answer because he offered no empathy for Job's plight. Neither did he express appreciation for Job's transparency regarding his suffering. Instead, Bildad insisted on informing Job his sons perished because of their own sins, which made him seem uncaring.

Rigidity. Another one of Job's friends, Eliphaz, was convinced these tragedies befell Job because of *his* own sins. Listen to Eliphaz's religious part: "Consider now. Who, being innocent, has ever perished? Where were the upright ever destroyed? As I have observed, those who plow evil and those who sow trouble reap it" (Job 4:7-8).

Religious parts often cling to a dichotomous view of the world. They live by the assumption that if you are innocent, your life would be pain-free. But if not? You must have broken God's law somewhere.

Tenacity. Scrutinize the entire forty-two chapters in the book bearing Job's name and you will see how persistent religious parts can be. Despite Job's vigorous self-defense, his three friends insisted it was impossible for him to live pure and still suffer losses.

Their perseverance is one reason it is best to avoid a power struggle with religious parts. We will talk about how to deal with them later.

Negativity. One reason religious parts present foolproof logic is to protect us from emotional flooding. But in doing so, they also inflict emotional damages. Job himself complained to his friends that they were "miserable comforters" (Job 16:2).

Bottom line, if someone quotes the Bible or uses God as an authority—but hurts your grieving heart in the process—a religious part might have incited the person.

POSITIVE INTENTIONS

The religious leaders in Jesus' days rejected him as the promised Messiah. Because Jesus healed the sick on the Sabbath, hobnobbed with tax collectors and prostitutes, even dared to call God his own father, they charged him with being a lawbreaker. It was as though they intentionally dismissed the miracles Jesus did and the Old Testament prophecies concerning the Messiah that were fulfilled in his life.

Convinced they were right, the Pharisees plotted and schemed to kill Jesus—and eventually succeeded after one of the twelve disciples, Judas Iscariot, betrayed him. Can anything good be said about the most well-known people with religious parts?

The Chosen thinks so. This show conveys Jesus' life from the perspective of those who interacted with him, including the religious leaders of his day. Since the actual Pharisees were driven by their religious parts, the TV show's Pharisees are no different. Gleaning insights from the actors who played these roles can help us better understand the nature of religious parts. Why do they seem blinded to human suffering?

Consider how Steve Shermett (who plays Rabbi Josiah in the show) describes Pharisees as a group: "They preserve the faith

. . . they're watching out for people who may be breaking God's law . . . prophets needed to be examined. It's the responsibility of the leadership, the Pharisees, to examine [Jesus] and see if his claims are true."[1] And according to Shaan Sharma (who plays Rabbi Shmuel), his character wanted a "strict adherence to the old ways, and not [be] quick to jump into something new, just because someone came along professing to be the Messiah."[2]

These talented actors illustrate religious parts' tenacity to serve as spiritual gatekeepers. Our religious parts revere God. They place his Word on a lofty pedestal. They carry an unshakeable devotion to keep us from trading God in for anything else. Loyal to teachings we learned in childhood, when they get a whiff of anything remotely disparaging to God, religious parts are quick to defend him.

OBJECTIONS TO GRIEF

It makes sense for our most religious parts to fight for God. But why would they fight us on grieving? Because they loathe displeasing God or dishonoring the Bible. This explains why Christians with strong religious parts often say we don't grieve like those "who have no hope" (1 Thessalonians 4:13) when they deem a fellow believer's grief to be excessive or otherwise inappropriate.

I once watched a renowned evangelist speak soon after the unexpected death of a minister friend he had known for decades. Their rich friendship explained the man's visible grief. Yet he was also quick to assert how Christians were not to respond with sadness when a loved one died. He cited the King James translation of Isaiah 53:4 as proof: "Surely [Jesus] has borne our griefs, and carried our sorrows."

Because Jesus has, indeed, carried our griefs and sorrows on the cross, religious parts like to argue that we have zero biblical basis to be grief-stricken.

BIBLICAL RESPONSES TO RELIGIOUS PARTS

The Bible does *not* ban grieving. On the contrary, God's own Son pronounced a blessing on those who mourn (Matthew 5:4). God *will* wipe away every tear from our eyes; but this blessed reality is reserved for a new heaven and earth, where "there will be no more death or mourning or crying or pain, for the old order of things has passed away" (Revelation 21:4).

We are not there yet—and God knows it. His response to our earthbound existence, with its "many trials and sorrows" (John 16:33 NLT), is to collect our tears in his bottle (Psalm 56:8 NLT). Maybe this is why the apostle Paul did not instruct us to scold mourners, but rather to "weep with those who weep" (Romans 12:15 NLT).

But what about Nehemiah 8:10? This verse plainly states, "Do not grieve, for the joy of the LORD is your strength." Reading verse 10 in isolation makes it seem we are forbidden to grieve at all times. But when we consider the context, another explanation emerges. The book of Nehemiah centers on the rebuilding of Jerusalem. Its walls needed restoring because the Israelites had strayed far from God. After his numerous attempts to correct them fell on deaf ears, the Almighty gave them over to their enemy, who ended up ransacking the Jewish people's sacred temple, destroying Jerusalem, and exiling them to Babylon.

Nehemiah 8 starts off with the leaders reading the law of Moses out loud, something we can safely assume never happened while they were living as exiles. The crowd started weeping after the Levites explained what they had just read. It could have been nostalgia; it could have been guilt for breaking the commandments. Regardless, Nehemiah instructed them to stop grieving that day: "This day is holy to the LORD your God. Do not mourn or weep" (Nehemiah 8:9). The Levites repeated the same instruction, almost verbatim, a couple of verses later: "Be still, for this is a holy day. Do not grieve" (Nehemiah 8:11).

Do you see the sandwich created by Nehemiah 8:9-11? Both verses 9 and 11 stress how the ban on grieving, verse 10, was only valid for that particular day.

God never demands for us to forgo grieving in general. Rather, he told his people to stop grieving for one singular day, because the day was sanctified.

Now, let's look at Isaiah 53:4, "Surely [Jesus] has borne our griefs, and carried our sorrows." The KJV translates the verse as Jesus bearing our griefs (Hebrew *choli*) and sorrows. However, *choli* is better translated as sickness.[3] Sorrows—*makob* in Hebrew—means pain, both physical and mental.[4] Other translations express the same verse as "surely [Jesus] took up our pain and bore our suffering" (NIV); "it was our sicknesses that He Himself bore, and our pains that He carried" (NASB). The Septuagint, the Greek translation of the Hebrew Bible, translated the verse as "He bears our sins, and is pained for us." Matthew 8:17, quoting from Isaiah 53:4, also expresses the idea of Jesus shouldering our infirmities and diseases.

In short, like these other translations show, we are *not* to understand Isaiah 53:4 as a divine edict against grieving.

PAUL'S RELIGIOUS PART

Paul, one of the Bible's most renowned Pharisees, descended from forefathers who were also Pharisees (Acts 23:6). He hunted Christians down, hauled them to prison, and voted to have them killed (Acts 8:3; 26:10-11). Paul had so much vitriol back then that the Bible says he "breathed out murderous threats against the Lord's disciples" (Acts 9:1).

But he could only continue such conduct until Jesus seized his attention supernaturally (Acts 9:3-19).

It is impossible to encounter the living God and emerge unchanged. The Bible records scores of people whose lives were radically transformed after meeting the Lord. Just ask Paul. The man who used to chase Jesus' followers with a vengeance ended up promoting their cause with as much passion. Now Paul preached *for* Jesus, with signs, wonders, and miracles (2 Corinthians 12:12), despite the intense persecution he faced (2 Corinthians 11:25). But please notice how Paul explained his past: "I thought to myself that I had to act in strong opposition to the name of Jesus of Nazareth" (Acts 26:9 NASB).

I submit Paul spoke these words while blended with his religious part.

For one thing, most of the Pharisees rejected Jesus. As a card-carrying member of that exclusive club, Paul would have had a zealous religious part that resonated with their stance. But the way Paul worded his description also hinted at his religious part's close presence. Since religious parts are a division of thinking parts, it makes sense for Paul to say "I *thought* to myself" if he was, indeed, blended with this part.

Paul's persecution of Christians was a clear case of spiritual warfare (Ephesians 6:10-12; 2 Corinthians 10:3-6). But it also happened because his religious part provoked him to do so.

Meeting Jesus, however, convicted the part of its error.

What happened to Paul's part is not a fluke. Hearing from God has the potential of changing not just us, but also our parts—including the most religious ones.

DIPPING INSIDE

Before your religious part can be transformed, we have to first find it. You can do so by calling to mind the loss in your life and its significance. Then, ask inside, *Is there any part that thinks I might be displeasing God? Please come forward so we can discuss it.*

Wait for what unfolds.

Once your religious part shows up—whether visually in your mind's eye, auditorily in a strong Scriptural stance on the inside, or by some other way that makes you know you are talking to your religious part—check how you feel toward it. If the answer is any of the 8 C's, send it to this part wherever you sense its presence. If not, ask any other part that might be blended with you to open up space so you can be alone with your religious part.

If your religious part welcomes your presence, ask the following and write the answers down.

What do you do for me in general?

_____

_____

_____

_____

What about in the context of my grief?

_____

_____

_____

_____

Are you concerned something bad might happen to me if you stopped doing your job? What might that be?

_____

_____

_____

_____

If you think I might displease God, please tell me why.

Clarify anything you do not fully comprehend with your part. But if you understand where your religious part is coming from, please express your appreciation to the part.

How does it respond? Note it here.

Let your part know the following: according to John 3:16, God loves people. But according to 1 Thessalonians 5:23, he created people with souls. This means God loves us *and* every part of our souls, including parts that are grieving.

Can your part apply this verse in the context of your grieving parts? That is, will the religious part let you help the parts of you that are missing the deceased, feeling helpless or scared about the future? In short, will it let you help your grieving parts?

If you sense an affirmative answer, thank the part. But if you don't, ask it, *What do you need from me or God before you'll let me help my exiles with their grief?* Jot any answer you sense.

We saw how an encounter with the Lord can change people *and* parts. God can show our parts the destiny he intends for them and whether they are on track—or if they are at risk of missing their calling. So if your part is agreeable, invite God to come. Ask the Lord, "What did you create my religious part for? What is your dream for it?"

Do you sense God's answer? Write it down and relay it to the part. How does your part respond?

Ask the Lord what you and your part need to do so it can live out God's dream for it. Write down God's answer.

Has your religious part been carrying a burden? Maybe it was passed down by your parents, pastors, or church. A yes deserves a follow-up; ask if it would like to release this burden if it knows it won't displease God by doing so. If your part is hesitant, remind it we have a standing invitation to cast our burdens to God, according to Matthew 11:28 and Psalm 55:22.

Once your part warms up to the idea, ask it to release this inherited burden. When the part is ready to do so, hand all of it to God.

_____

_____

_____

_____

Would your part like to replace the burden with any positive quality? This can be anything good that will help you cope with the loss, be it spiritual in nature (like the fruit of the Spirit, Galatians 5:22-23) or otherwise (such as "a pleasant disposition"). If so, ask the Lord to give your part these qualities.

_____

_____

_____

_____

If there is nothing more your religious part would like to share with you (or ask of you), please send a heartfelt appreciation for your part. I recommend setting an intention to check in with this part in the weeks to come, so that it will not feel alone.

7

Firefighters

YOUR OWN PAINKILLERS

WITHIN TWENTY-FOUR HOURS after hearing about Matthew
Perry's death, sadness had saturated me. My thinking part re-
garded this development with interest: *Such a strong response*!

I affirmed this part's reaction. After all, I did not work in the
entertainment industry nor had the privilege of knowing the
actor personally. So why did his passing affect me?

After communicating my curiosity inward, my sad parts explained how hearing about the actor's sudden death brought back
the shocking time following my own unexpected loss. But they
were also saddened because the actor's most famous role was the
lovable Chandler Bing of *Friends* (1994–2004). *Feels like losing a
friend*, my parts explained, echoing Perry's other fans.[1]

For one solid week following the actor's tragic demise, *Friends*
became America's most watched TV program.[2] His fans picked a
brilliant way to cope. As you will soon see, firefighter parts strive
to soften the grueling task of grieving by anesthetizing us, including by using entertainment and humor.

FIREFIGHTER PARTS IN ACTION

How about you? What is your go-to solution when stressed out?

No, I am not necessarily referring to creams or chemicals. Your favorite painkillers can be anything that soothes you against the problem at hand—or in this case, distracts you from reminders of your loss.

I have a firefighter that stuffs my grocery cart with Lay's Original Kettle Cooked chips, four yellow bags at a time. (My inner critic wants the record to show how it has relentlessly railed against these sorry excuses for food—and that it will continue to do so.) In contrast, your firefighter may be on the lookout for sugar, like a pint of cookies and cream. A pan of warm, gooey brownies. Or both.

But maybe you prefer to work out. In that case, your firefighter might urge you to lace up your sneakers for a bone-tiring run. If your muscles are so exhausted you cannot think of anything, much less feel the loss you suffered, mission accomplished.

If you swear by so-called retail therapy, you might sense an increased impulse to shop. The thrill of selecting something shiny can soften some of the ache you feel inside.

Digital natives might simultaneously overwork their thumbs and numb their minds as they scroll through scores of social media posts. Others spend every possible moment in immersive online games.

Some other firefighters might douse the pain of grief with ciga-rettes. Chemicals. Sex.

J. William Worden, who wrote the handbook *Grief Counseling and Grief Therapy*, recounted a story about a widower who married his second wife immediately after burying his first. Guess where he met the woman? At his first wife's memorial service.[3] This widower must have had manager parts—who strategized with firefighter parts—to douse his grief. Their scheme? To marry him off to the first suitable candidate they could attract.

Can you see these parts high-fiving each other at his wedding? *Good job, everybody!*

But maybe your grief is not about the loss of a significant other at all. Still, if you approach your firefighters with curiosity, they will likely confirm their mission for you—which is to sedate you from feeling the sorrow in your system. It only takes a whiff of pain to set firefighters off, dousing the flame of emotions at all costs.

At. All. Costs. Like their human counterparts, firefighter parts will stop at nothing to protect us. No sharp reprimands, shaming strategies, or severe threats can coax them to abdicate their responsibility. Firefighter parts are indifferent about all of the above. If they are convinced the weight of your grief might bury you alive, they will distract, numb, and lure you to engage in any number of tactics—including self-destructive ones—to veer you far away from such agony.

But let your internal team of dedicated firefighters know, avoiding grief cannot permanently reduce your misery. Dr. Lisa Shulman, a neurologist whose husband died, wrote about grief this way: "Accumulating evidence shows that avoidance of reminders of loss doesn't reduce emotional distress. . . . On the contrary, exposure to painful emotions and memories is a difficult but necessary step on the path of healing."[4]

If you detect heavy skepticism in your firefighters despite this feedback, hang on. Here comes another way to help them.

THE PAIN IN PAINKILLERS

Matthew Perry revealed his longtime struggle with addiction and emotional pain in a memoir published only one year prior to his demise. The actor's autobiography corroborates how deeply

Perry struggled with unmet emotional desires.[5] His parents divorced when he was a mere infant, forcing him to split his childhood between Canada and the United States. He did not feel at home with either parent's new family. As an adult, Perry cycled through repeated efforts to woo women, only to leave them before they had the chance to leave him. His lonely love life caused *Rolling Stone* to label him as "commitment phobic."[6] Perry died as a never-married bachelor.

But the piece of his history that pierces my heart each time I ponder it has to do with how his parents flew him from Montreal to Los Angeles by himself—get this—at age 5, which left him terrified.

Can we pause? Let's grasp the enormity of what those young shoulders had to bear. Flying can be intimidating to begin with. But to fly internationally? Alone? As a child? Surrounded by towering adults and unfamiliar faces? *Of course,* he felt scared.

What a burden of aloneness—and longing—to drag into adulthood. No wonder his profile on Twitter (now X) reads, "Extremely skilled poet and dancer with *a seemingly endless sense of longing.* Hi!"[7] (emphasis added).

Granted, Perry was an outstanding comic. Perhaps he fashioned the italicized line strictly for laughs. If so, we should not read into his public declaration of having a "strong desire especially for something unattainable," which is how Merriam-Webster defines *longing.*

However, as his memoir exposes, that pithy line also reveals a painful truth. You cannot read his words without realizing how poignant an illustration his life was. Chapter after chapter paints the unbreakable bond between exiles—parts holding hurtful memories—and firefighters. The deeper the hurt, the fiercer the protection. Even if it means suffering from an entrenched addiction.

By the end of his memoir, Perry's firefighters had quieted down, allowing him to maintain sobriety. He credited God for this transformation. His kitchen encounter with the Almighty left him feeling taken care of and safe.[8]

How I wish we could wrap up his story right there. But the talented actor, who brought so much joy to so many, did not leave on a lighthearted note. Perry fell back into addiction and died from a ketamine overdose.[9]

But still. Learning about his encounter with God emboldened my hope that one day I can scour heaven for him, pump his hand, and thank him for bringing us Chandler Bing. Maybe he is charming heavenly residents with witty one-liners even now.

What could *be* more delightful?

NUMBING AND DISSOCIATIVE PARTS

Addictive substances are only one among firefighters' many tools to protect us from grief. *Addiction* comes from the Latin word which suggests "being literally given over to something in devotion."[10] As we have seen before, in their furious attempt to shield us from emotional flames, firefighters will entice us to devote our attention to anything other than the pain. But if their efforts fail, you can expect them to deploy two other tactics: numbing and dissociation. Some people have relied on substances to numb their pain; but a firefighter part can numb us emotionally without the use of any substance. For instance, experiencing trauma can make some survivors feel nothing—numb.

If you have ever endured an invasive medical procedure which required some form of anesthesia, you know the bliss that physical numbness offers. The surgeon can stick his sharp instrument into your soft tissues and even slice them here and there, but as far as you are concerned, no pain is registering. Likewise, firefighter parts can resort to numbing us mentally, shielding us from grief's piercing emotions.

What about dissociation? Some describe this phenomenon as an out-of-body experience: the sensation that you are watching yourself—as though from a vantage point outside your body—as something unpleasant is happening. Another example of dissociation is when you tune out the conversations around you. And if you have ever lost track of time—say, while driving down a familiar route—chances are, it happened because you dissociated.

You will soon have the opportunity to befriend your firefighters, including any numbing or dissociative part. But they are unlikely to stand down unless we circle back to a part we have previously met. So let's head there first.

CRITICS REVISITED

Firefighter parts will attempt to soothe us at *all* costs. They will employ their best effort regardless of whether their suggestion is actually detrimental for you. For example, if your loss is so debilitating it keeps you from returning to work, you might sense an urge to smoke marijuana and soar above the pain. But if you then hear a stern "voice" in your head—*Shame on you for being a pot head! What would your Bible study group say if they saw you like this?*—that is your inner critic, pouncing on your firefighters to cease and desist.

Critics are often polarized with firefighters. Just as my critic has been waging a war against my chips-hoarding firefighter, it is probable for your critic to run a campaign against your firefighters. So as we turn our attention to your inner world, please ask your critic to come first.

DIPPING INSIDE

Tell your critic what you have observed: (select the relevant fire-fighting activities) overeating, spending excessive time online, playing video games for hours, watching movies non-stop, cutting or other self-harming behavior, maxing out your credit cards, getting high, vaping, smoking, sleeping around, driving at high speeds, or any other activity along the same vein.

Keeping your heart open toward your critic, ask it, *Do you realize that by criticizing me, you are also provoking my firefighters?* Jot down its response.

_____

_____

_____

_____

If need be, assure your critic that you see its point about your firefighters' recklessness.

_____

_____

_____

_____

If you promise to be present throughout the grieving process, is your critic willing to soften its criticisms so your firefighters could similarly unwind?

_____

_____

_____

_____

Ask your critic, *Is there anything else you want me to know?* Listen
to its answer and thank the critic for its willingness to chat.

_____

_____

_____

_____

Take a deep breath. Well done!

Now, let's find the parts that are responsible for the above fire-
fighting activities. Locate them in or around your body. Once you
find them, notice their shape, size, color, movement, and so on.
You can focus on one firefighter part at a time or work with them
as a group.

_____

_____

_____

_____

Did your firefighters hear the conversation you had with your
critic? If yes, invite their feedback.

_____

_____

_____

_____

Your firefighters want the best for you. Knowing this, how do you feel toward them? If the answer is one of the 8 C's, send it to them and see how they respond. (If you feel anything but the 8 C's, it means you're blended with another part, maybe even the critic. Keep asking any blended part to make space until you genuinely feel one of the 8 C's toward your firefighters.)

_____

_____

_____

_____

Ask your firefighters, *Do you trust I'll be okay even when dealing with grief?*

_____

_____

_____

_____

If you detect hesitation, it can help to update parts with your current age. (For instance, *I am now an adult. Does this fact help you trust me more?*) Show them snippets of the times you managed to survive intense emotions. Tell your firefighters: *Emotions did not—and will not—kill me. Plus, I can ask my exiles not to flood me.*

How do your firefighters respond?

_____

_____

_____

_____

If your background contains trauma—including because the loss you are mourning was due to violence—or if you have a dissociative part, it might help to see a therapist. Having another person hold space for you lends ease to the work. That is because when someone is holding space for you, that person is offering an undivided attention and support as you focus on your internal world.

See if your parts have any reaction to you finding your own IFS therapist.

_____

_____

_____

_____

Now, let's give a shout out for numbing parts. Numbness following death and loss often fades as time goes by. But if it has been a while since your loss happened and you still feel numb about the loss, ask for space from the part that numbs you. If you sense resistance, ask it, *Why are you reluctant to give me space? What do you fear might happen?*

_____

_____

_____

_____

Address this part's fear if you can. For instance, assure the part you can withstand emotions, including painful ones. Notice the impact of your assurance on this part.

_____

_____

Please also appreciate what your numbing part is trying to accomplish. Its aim is to protect you.

Is this part interested in learning a better way to achieve its goal? If you sense a yes, let it know Jesus is also known as Prince of Peace (Isaiah 9:6). This means wherever Jesus is, there is also peace. He can keep your parts functioning without having to lock anyone in a frozen state. Can your numbing part trust that when we partner with Jesus, you and every part of you will be safe—regardless of the emotions that might be stirred up? This way, your numbing part can take a break from having to numb you as a form of protection. It can watch Jesus doing the work to protect you as you help your parts grieve.

After you ask the question, do not think up the answer. Just wait for your part to respond. If the part is still hesitant, maybe this part is not fully aware of who the Son of God truly is. Invite it to get to know Jesus with you as you read the Bible and pray in times to come.

Now, let's return to your firefighters as a group. Please ask them, *May I help you with your own grief?* If they agree, please help your parts accordingly. Even the act of listening to their grief is helpful.

Finally, send an appreciation to your hardworking firefighters. Thank them for spending time with you.

PART 3

Exiles

Shock

OODLES OF LOOSE ENDS

"Papa is no longer here!"

My mom's call shattered what had been a peaceful Friday. Except it was already Saturday for my mother, who called from Jakarta.

So Papa left. Why does Mama sound so frantic? Confused, I asked her to clarify. "If he's not there, then where did he go?"

I did not know it then, but her answer wound up decimating more than just my evening.

After their kids grew up and left, my parents developed the same routine each weekend: Sundays were reserved for God and church. But on Saturdays, Papa would drop Mama off at her hair salon before playing tennis at their local sports club. My father loved tennis.

That particular Saturday saw my parents starting their usual weekend rhythm. But the ordinary day turned unforgettable the moment a phone call reached Mama. She learned that Papa had been rushed to the nearest clinic because of "an accident" at the sports club. Someone who worked at the salon raced my mother to the clinic.

There he was! Lying on the doctor's examination bed in his workout attire, Papa appeared exactly as she had last seen him. But his eyes were shut and he was still.

Perhaps he fell asleep, she thought. *Has the doctor finished examining him?* Mama shook Papa's shoulders.

No response.

She shook him again. Harder.

Why wouldn't he stir?

Panicking now, Mama started shrieking. "Papa! Papa! Wake up! It's me!"

She quit only after a clinic staffer gently broke the news that he was "no longer here."

Mama must have called me while the phrase still riddled her mind. No wonder hysteria trickled through the miles separating us.

"He's no longer here, Audrey. Your father has died."

After we buried him, I interviewed my father's doubles tennis partner about the final moments of Papa's life. The man described there was no accident that claimed his life. Instead, Papa's heart gave out as he was about to serve their opponent.

Papa was athletic all his life. Name a sport and he would have at least tried it: Swimming. Golf. Bowling. Tennis and table tennis. He even won the national badminton youth championship while in college.

I had just said goodbye to my parents a couple weeks prior. We were making holiday plans. "Please return this December," I pleaded.

He left it at "We'll see."

Papa's cryptic answer echoed in my mind as Mama ended the call.

My father was smart. Handsome. But also, down to earth. He treated everyone with the same kind respect, whether they were a millionaire or moneyless. He was the quintessential family man. He remembered extended family members' birthdays—no small feat, given his enormous family tree—and called his many cousins and elders on a regular basis to catch up. He loved hosting family for get-togethers. He often concluded his trips abroad by buying gifts for his relatives.

Indeed, Papa was generous. Born the third in a family of eleven, my dad put himself through college. Prior to their wedding day, Papa informed Mama he wished to send a portion of his salary to his younger siblings so they all could complete their studies. My father willingly loaned money to those who were hard-pressed. It did not matter if they worked for him, if they knew him from church, or even if they were strangers. To this day, there are a couple of masseuses in Jakarta who have yet to return the money he loaned them.

One of my most cherished memories of Papa was how he used to sing songs to my toddler self as we ambled by the river each morning. When I was older, I noticed how he would whistle back at the twittering birds, trying to trick them into thinking this oversized creature was somehow speaking their language.

The man taught me to ride a bike and to drive stick shift. Having him as a father bestowed me with so much treasure—living with integrity, the winsomeness of staying humble, a passion for psychology and people, the joy of watching the Indonesian badminton team cream their opponents, a lifelong hankering for *pempek*[1] and the distinctive fish chips from his hometown—

He *died*?

The notion sounded so incredulous, my mom might as well have said, *Your dad jumped on a one-way train to Jupiter.*

SUDDEN LOSS AND UNANSWERED QUESTIONS

Goodbyes are hard. Even if you can sense them coming—whether in the case of a physical death or any other type of ending—the resulting grief is not necessarily easy to bear. Just because you can anticipate your loss does not mean you will hurt less.

With an unforeseen loss, however, an additional, complicating component often occurs. That is because unexpected loss adds shock and its related stress to our grief. Having to suddenly shift our perspective, from business-as-usual to suddenly bereft, can leave some of our parts disoriented.

I wonder if you have uttered sentiments similar to the following:

Could I have done more to keep this divorce from happening?

If only I had kept my temper, it might've prevented his fatal stroke.

The fire destroyed everything. What now?

Why didn't I implore him to see the doctor sooner?

How can I pay the mortgage and provide for the kids all by myself?

You might worry whether the person who died harbored any ill will against you, especially if it happened right after you exchanged tense words with the departed. If you have to downsize or make major decisions you are unsure the deceased would have approved of, you might feel insecure. If you suddenly lost your job, the fear of becoming homeless might feel too threatening to consider.

Because it is painful to simmer in them, our protector parts prefer to keep us far from reflecting on the loose ends associated with unexpected loss. Scripture says, "Anxiety weighs down the heart" (Proverbs 12:25). Accordingly, left unchecked, these introspective inquiries can crash us into depression and self-blame.

Thankfully, there is a safe way to attend to your unexpected loss. The key is to be Self-led. Remember the 8 C's that define your Self? By being courageous, for instance, you can approach parts that are burdened with the suddenness of your loss and negotiate: if they agree not to flood you with all of their what-ifs and if-onlys, you can help them tie up loose ends. You can also maintain curiosity about your introspection.

This is what I mean. Soon after my father died, I noticed the same question reappearing within me: *Papa, how could you have left like this?* It was the deep longing to hear the answer that birthed the following IFS session.

IFS: NOT SÉANCE

But before we get there, let's begin with a preface: what you are about to read is an emotional, not spiritual, experience. I connected with my father in a psychotherapy session—*not* in a spiritually questionable meeting.

Scripture is clear. We are *not* to contact the dead through mediums, psychics, and the like (Leviticus 20:5-7; Isaiah 8:19-20). Further, King Saul perished in the battlefield partly because he summoned the late prophet Samuel through a medium (1 Samuel 28:3-25; 1 Chronicles 10:12-14). I have absolutely *no* desire to do IFS if it means displeasing the God I love.

My religious part knew about the above Scriptures; it also knew my heart's motivation to follow God fully. Still, it voiced its objection against using IFS to convey my sentiments to my father.

Taking the time to address this part's objection helped it to relax. But if the part had not, I would not have badgered it until it gave in. I would have abandoned my desire to talk to my father instead.

Now, let's bring it back to you. If you share my religious part's objection, please heed it. You can also see if it shifts its position after reading this chapter. If not, chapter eleven offers you another effective way to connect—emotionally speaking—with your departed loved one.

MY IFS SESSION

After hearing from my religious part, I sensed this part's intention was to keep me from incurring God's wrath by reconnecting with my late father. I asked my part if this was accurate. The part confirmed it.

Maybe I'll pray first. This thought calmed my religious part, so I closed my eyes. "Lord Jesus, is it okay if I communicate with Papa in my mind's eye? Please let me know. Amen."

Hearing this prayer activated my thinking part. I saw a mental picture of someone with both hands up, as though flabbergasted. *Of course it's okay! The conversation is only in your mind. It's not like you'll be conducting a séance.*

I thanked my thinking part for chiming in and asked it to give me space. In response, I felt increased peace, which meant the thinking part receded from my awareness.

Then, a series of scenes unfolded. Jesus, clad in a white robe, appeared to my right. He assured me it's fine to invite my father to join my inner dialogue. Then the Lord slipped behind a curtain. In the same way you can instinctively understand things in a dream just by watching it play out, I sensed Jesus did this to keep me from feeling self-conscious.

I was still marveling at the Lord's gracious gesture when I became aware of my father. Although the space we shared was shadowy, I detected he wore a polo shirt, shorts, and sneakers, as if ready for a tennis match. We were flanked by white hexagonal porcelain stools with intricate blue swirls.

Sitting cross-legged on the ground, I rested against my stool. Papa sat on his about ten feet away.

"I miss you," I told Papa.

"I know," he replied. Papa advised me to enjoy my time on earth and not leave early.

His mention of dying early revived my curiosity. "Why did *you* leave early, Papa?"

Pat answers like "God called him home" did nothing to satisfy my quest for the truth. The timing of his passing could not have been God's doing because God is not the author of confusion or disorder (1 Corinthians 14:33). Yet, my father's death discombobulated our family and the company he started; I took an open-ended leave from my practice and lost all my clients; my mom had to scramble with arrangements after his death. Later, Mama confided how it was solely God's fierce grace that sustained her through those trying days.

The anguish in Papa's response to my inquiry was palpable: "I thought I had more time."

POST-SESSION POSTSCRIPTS

What you have just read did *not* result from my creative effort to compose an evocative dialogue. My graduate training equipped me to work with souls, not screenplays. But since I did not make up the session and it was not my late father's spirit that appeared, then where did the vision of my father come from?

One plausible answer: my neurons.

In her book, *The Grieving Brain*, Dr. Mary-Frances O'Connor, a neuroscientist and psychologist, explains, "It is *because your loved one existed* that certain neurons fire together and certain proteins are folded in your brain in particular ways. It is because your loved one lived, and because you loved each other, that means when the person is no longer in the outer world, they still physically exist—in the wiring of the neurons of your brain" (emphasis in the original).[2] She explains in an interview, "I have loved this person [who died], my own physical brain is different, thus I carry them literally in my brain."[3] Perhaps when we communicate with our departed loved ones via IFS, we are getting in touch with the version of the person stored in our neurons.

But the process itself unfolds unconsciously. For instance, the back and forth between my father and myself felt natural, as though I was truly communicating with another person—albeit through sensing (instead of audibly hearing) his thoughts. During the session I felt more freedom to share candidly from my heart than when he was still earthbound. My father's responses also felt emotionally richer.

Even though seeing Papa in an IFS session did not change the circumstance—our family still had to dig through the rubble and rebuild—the part of me which was burdened by his abrupt departure has since breathed easier. This part believes Papa was as unprepared by the suddenness of his own ending as we were.

DIPPING INSIDE

If you yelled at your sister before the accident that claimed her life, a part might crave her forgiveness. If a cousin killed himself, there might be a part yearning to hear if he thought you cared for him enough. If your child went missing, you may have a ton of things you wish you could share with the apple of your eye.

You now have the opportunity to listen to parts of you that might be bothered by how your loss resulted in loose ends.

However, just because I had a part longing to communicate with my late father does not mean you have a similar part. Your inner world might need something different. To discover what that might be, focus internally. Ask inside, *Is there a part concerned about the loose ends after my loss?* If you sense a yes, notice what unfolds.

_____

_____

_____

_____

See or sense how many parts show up. If there are more than one, ask them to group themselves based on similarities. For instance, ask all parts that are unsure about what to do with grief's messy aftermath to stand together. If you find other parts—like ones feeling fearful, resentful, or sad—let them know you will connect with them later. Since other chapters in this book will help you with these parts, ask them to wait for their turns.

If all of your parts listen to your request, you will be left with a group of parts that feel unsure about what to do. Please focus on that group for the next section.

PROMPTS FOR YOUR PARTS

How do you notice these parts? Write down the number of parts that showed up, as well as their shapes, thoughts, feelings, or how they make your body feel—for instance, by doubling your heart rate or causing tingles to race down your arms.

_____

_____

_____

_____

How do you feel toward this group of parts? Is there curiosity or compassion for them? If not, another part might be nearby. Ask any such part to make space.

_____

_____

_____

_____

Keep repeating the above step until you feel an openness toward the target group of parts. Share your openness, compassion, or curiosity with them.

If you sense receptivity, ask them to explain, one by one, how they are doing since the loss happened. Listen to every part and write their answers down.

_____

_____

_____

_____

Is your heart moved by the struggle you hear? Then share your reaction with them. Let them know you are here and therefore, they are not alone. Notice how your parts respond.

_____

_____

_____

_____

Does this group of parts need anything from you to help them grieve? Don't think up the answer. Wait for their response.

List everything this group of parts needs from you.

_____

_____

_____

_____

Please do your best to fulfill their requests. But for the sake of trust building, only promise what you can deliver to your parts.

Are any of your parts curious about talking to the deceased within an IFS session? In my experience, it is best to do so while someone else is holding the space for you. Your Self energy, combined with a skilled IFS therapist's Self energy, can facilitate the interaction more smoothly. So see how your inner system feels about partnering with an IFS professional to help your grieving process.

_____

_____

_____

_____

If this group of parts has nothing more to share or ask of you, thank them. Set an intention to check back with them in the near future if it feels right to do so.

Sadness and Sorrow

LIKE A MANGOSTEEN STAIN

SADNESS IS THE MOST COMMON FEELING in bereavement.[1] No surprise here. At the heart of grieving is sorrow over lost love. As Francis Weller said, "Grief is akin to praise; it is how the soul recounts the depth to which someone has touched our lives."[2]

C. S. Lewis compared the grief of burying his wife to surviving an amputation. He claimed that even if he learned to stump around with a wooden leg, the reality of losing that leg would never recede. Listen to his grim conclusion: "I shall never be a biped again."[3]

Sadness tends to linger, just like the stain from mangosteen.

Mango *what*?

Loaded with antioxidants and vitamins, this tropical fruit looks like a purple orb on the outside with stark white flesh on the inside. In case you plan on trying one, let me pass on a warning: watch out for the juice. If you let any trickle onto your clothes, the stain *will* stay—even if its intensity will fade over time.

Even though my mother taught me as much, the first time I cracked open a mangosteen shell, my shirt bore the reminder of the fruit that bled on me.

How can your soul do any less with the loss you suffered?

THE STICKINESS OF SADNESS

Sadness is difficult to digest, partly because loss affects multiple facets of our lives.

Divorce is an example. The demise of your marriage might have also forced you to relocate—which means leaving behind your house, friendly neighbors, favorite diner, and so on. Having to put your poodle to sleep means you are also losing an endless source of unconditional love, pure joy, and the camaraderie of other dog parents.

Tabitha was stunned when church members she considered friends stopped socializing with her after her husband's death. Because her husband pastored their church, after he died she also lost the parsonage, her income, and her spiritual community, because she eventually moved to another church.

But that was not all. Because Tabitha got married in her early 20s, almost her entire adulthood was intertwined with him and his job. She always considered herself a pastor's wife. Who was she now? Losing her husband resulted in multiple reasons for Tabitha's sadness to linger.

Sadness is also hard to grapple with because allowing it to surface seems self-defeating. Unlike excitement, sadness does not pump us with the energy to face the day. Sadness cannot convince the faucets of our brains to drip endorphins the way happiness and love can. Expressing sadness in the presence of another is risky; the listener can change the subject, beat a hasty retreat, or attempt to cheer us up—which can make us feel as though we do not have the permission to be sad.[4]

That is why some mourners try to suppress sadness, hoping the passing of time will dull the edge. But Jesse, who we met in chapter four, found this tactic to be faulty. Even though the loss of his grandmother had happened decades ago, nothing had diminished his grief.

NEGOTIATING ACCESS TO SADNESS

The last time we heard from Jesse, he connected with a part that prevented him from grieving Granny's death. I summarized the part's stance and asked him to clarify: "It seems this part internalized messages on how you shouldn't mourn Granny's death because she was only a step-grandparent. Is this accurate?"

"Yes," Jesse confirmed.

"Do you agree with these messages?" I asked him.

"Not really. Even though she was my step-grandmother, Granny was the only parental figure who spent time with me. We lived with Granny and Gramps until I was about 5, but Mom worked all the time and was hardly there. Granny used to let me play with Legos the entire day and made gooey chocolate chip cookies for me."

"Did your part hear this, Jesse?" I inquired. "Let it know how much Granny loved you."

Jesse took the time to connect with his part internally. Shoulders more relaxed, he sat back. "The part is more at ease," he reported. "But it's afraid if I get in touch with the sadness of losing Granny, I'd be too depressed and wouldn't be able to function."

"Understandable. But what if we set a time limit? Is there an amount of time you can spend with the sad part that won't feel overwhelming?"

"Ooh, this part likes that. It's saying ten minutes."

"Thank this part and ask the sad part to come—"

But before I finished, Jesse shook his head. "No. It's shameful to let the sad part express grief, especially visibly, like by crying."

"Who's saying this?" I pressed.

Jesse checked internally and returned with a report. "A part that remembers how Mom used to mock me for crying. The part also says my partner, Matt, didn't shed any tears after his dad died, so I shouldn't either."

"Is your heart open toward this part, Jesse?"

"Yep."

"Great. Show your open heart to your part and see how it responds."

After a period of silence, Jesse piped up. "My part appreciates it. I told my part that just because Matt didn't cry doesn't mean I have to grieve exactly like him."

"How did your part respond?"

"It said, *But what about your mom? She mocked you for crying. It must mean crying is bad.* I don't know how to respond to that."

"Just as our body will bleed if something sharp cuts it, crying is our heart's natural response when something breaks it. Besides that, your Mom isn't around. Nobody here will mock you if you end up with a few tears."

"My part is still a bit wary, but it's also willing to try."

"Excellent! Thank that part, please. And as you excuse it, let's also ask the sad part to come forward. I'll set the timer for ten minutes."

I waited for a few beats as Jesse tuned into his internal world. Then, a whisper broke the stillness. "Granny was the only person I felt unconditional support from. When she died, I lost my childhood. No more softness. I even lost Gramps too. He moved out of state, remarried, and stopped talking to us. It feels like a betrayal. The two people who loved me the most, left."

Jesse's sadness saturated the room. It felt appropriate for me to honor the moment with silence.

His voice cracking, Jesse stammered, "All my happy memories are connected to Granny. Now she's gone."

Toward the end of the ten-minute mark, I asked Jesse to let his sad part know he fully grasped the depth of the part's sorrow.

I also prompted him to check with the part if receiving Jesse's compassion helped in some way.

"The part felt helped, but it also needs more time with me."

"Let the part know you can schedule another visit with it, but we also need to keep the ten-minute agreement. Ask your part if it needs anything else from you."

After checking with the part, Jesse reported, "It said, *Don't judge me for being emotional even though Granny died a long time ago.*"

Jesse nodded his agreement.

INTERNAL TUG OF WAR

Because parts are diverse in their needs and level of hurt, parts work is best done by focusing on one part at a time. But what happens when you stumble on a polarized group of parts, like when a subgroup within your sad parts prefers to manifest their grief one way while another opposes this idea?

For example, one subgroup might insist on decorating your house for Christmas while another objects: *No way. You can't take your annual holiday picture. What about the daughter you've just buried?*

Please give both sides of the polarization equal attention. Imagine a wide enough space within your heart and position each group on either side of you. Ask both groups to tell you—not the other side—their concerns and needs. Listen with your heart. Send your compassion to both.

Once parts feel heard, they are typically willing to soften. So after verifying with both parties if they feel heard by you, see if a middle ground can satisfy them. Perhaps both subgroups will agree to a compromise. Or you may find one subgroup reverses its earlier stance.

DIPPING INSIDE

How about if we start the following segment by taking deep breaths? Keep going until you feel calm and present. This sensation lets your inner world know you are here, ready to engage your sad parts.

If there are protector parts around—perhaps hesitant to let you meet your sad parts—validate their concern. Sure, getting in touch with sadness may cause you to recall bittersweet memories of your deceased loved one, which has the potential to make you feel even sadder. But feeling sad (or any other emotion) has no power to kill you.

Check if your protectors can relax enough to let your sadness emerge. It may be useful to set a time limit to meet with your sad parts, especially if this is your first try. Having a time boundary can help your protectors relax.

Once they green-light your access, invite your sad parts in. You will know they have arrived when you sense an aura of anguish inside. Or maybe you start noticing memories related to your loss.

Ask your sad parts to focus on one thread at a time and to not overwhelm you. Which section of their sorrow would they like to share with you first? As you see or hear the answer, check your heart. Do you feel compassionate toward your sad parts? Let them feel it. Tell them they are not alone in their grief. Ask them, *Can you feel my presence?* Notice the effect of your open-hearted presence on them.

What else do they want to share about that particular thread of their sadness? Keep listening until they have shared everything on that topic. Remember, parts can use words, images, sensations, memories, feelings, or thoughts to communicate.

_____

_____

_____

Ask your parts, *Do you feel I get what you are sharing?* If you receive
a no, follow up. Ask, *What am I missing?* and listen for the response.

_____

_____

_____

If you are not getting a clear answer, there could be a part blocking
you from fully connecting with sadness. Glance inside your heart
and ask if there is part blocking your access. If so, ask its concerns
about letting you meet with the sad parts alone. Then, ask the
part for space. You will know this other part has left when you
feel more spacious or peaceful inside.

_____

_____

_____

Once this happens, return to the sad parts and ask, *Do you feel I
am getting all you want me to get?* If not, ask them to keep showing
you everything they are sad about until there is nothing more to
share or until they believe you fully understand them.

_____

_____

Then, invite them to unburden. *Would you like to release any burden related to your grief?* Instruct them to remove any emotion, belief, thoughts they do not wish to carry any more. There are different ways for parts to unburden: for instance, they can release their burden to water, light, fire, wind, or something else. They can also surrender their burden to God, who tends to us as gently as a mother nurses her newborn (Isaiah 49:15; 66:13).

While some choose to unburden physically, like burning love letters in a fireplace after a difficult divorce, unburdenings that happen in your mind's eye are just as powerful.

Once the process is completed, ask if your parts wish to invite essential qualities to replace these burdens. They can also ask the Lord for any gift to replace the burden with.

Jot them down.

Receive these qualities by breathing them in, one by one.

Check in with your unburdened parts on a regular basis for the next few weeks. This practice will help them settle into their unburdened state instead of readopting their old burden.

If you unburdened your sad parts, congratulations. But remember, they may have more threads on sadness to show you. Ask them if this is true—and if they would like an additional visit from you. If you are sensing a yes, set an intention to meet with them again.

If your parts refused to unburden, that is fine. We will get to what you can do about it in chapter fourteen.

Please thank your sad parts. Also thank other parts that stepped aside to allow you to meet with your sadness.

Christmas with Papa and Mama (Virginia Beach, Virginia). How I physically stood between my parents is the position you want to be when resolving tension between two polarized parts.

10

Anger and Rage

INCLUDING AT GOD

ASK CELEBRITIES THE FOLLOWING and the candid ones might concede: fame cannot guarantee a candy-sweet life. Take Kermit the Frog, for instance. His acting chops have entertained kids and adults for decades. His reputation hides no controversy. No drugs. No foul language. No scandal. Who doesn't adore this lovable creature?

Yet as he crooned in his song (with almost 10 million YouTube views!), "It's Not Easy Being Green." Turns out the world's famous frog favors yellow. And red. Being green means ordinary things—like leaves—can conceal him. But Kermit does not enjoy being overlooked.

Aww. Isn't his confession charming and relatable? We can all name something we dislike about ourselves. This includes my angry part, who once confided, *It's not easy being me*. But before I share more about this part, let me interject a request: compassion flows naturally when the object is a cuddly character like Kermit. But since angry parts are far less endearing, it takes intentionality to remain open-hearted as we delve into lesser-known facts about these parts.

So may I request for you to stay curious? Doing so will help you learn something new about your own part as we extend our angry parts the courtesy of curiosity.

Why would my angry part say it has a hard life?

The answer may have to do with multiple Bible verses which seem to vilify anger: "Stop being angry! Turn from your rage" (Psalm 37:8 NLT). "Don't hang out with angry people, don't keep company with hotheads" (Proverbs 22:24 MSG). Or how about this subtler one, "Stupid people express their anger openly" (Proverbs 29:11 GNT)? No wonder Christians often treat anger as though it were the Devil's nastier brother.

The thing is, anger is as valid a feeling as anguish, anticipation, or any other emotion. According to Dr. John Townsend, author and psychologist, "Feelings that are buried are always buried alive."[1] But buried feelings will tantrum when we force them to shush. They will create one scene after another to flag our attention. If we continue to ignore them—whether because we feel clumsy with handling emotions or because we have been socialized to avoid anger altogether—these buried feelings will escalate matters into a spectacular event.

And when this happens, others *will* witness our anger.

TOMAS'S ANGRY PART

Ever since his mother died, Tomas, a 37-year-old man, has been tending to his parts: sadness, sorrow, guilt. And then Tomas enrolled in a seminary—and encountered anger.

One instructor, Pastor Warren, taught the class to respect their parents' wishes. A host of Tomas's parts felt guilty because, despite being the first-born, he did not visit Mom in Mexico during the last few years of her life, even though she had asked him to.

Pastor Warren's lecture evoked Tomas's rage.

His angry part collected a mound of incriminating evidence against the pastor. First, considering his class was on leadership and *not* family, Pastor Warren overused the word *mom*. Besides, the angry part continued, the pastor deliberately glanced at him each time he mouthed the dreaded word.

That last statement planted a frown on Tomas's face. He doubted Pastor Warren would intentionally look his way, as though emphasizing a point while saying *mom*. At the same time, Tomas wondered if his part was correct about Pastor Warren's excessive use of the word. This conclusion drove him to confide in the pastor about how his inability to visit Mom made him feel awful; would Pastor Warren refrain from repeating *mom* so much, please?

But it was as though the conversation never happened. By the next lecture, *mom* kept rolling off the pastor's tongue. The angry part gloated at this development. Finally, proof that its wrath was justified! But its elation was short-lived. Every time the pastor said *mom*, Tomas's guilty parts heard it as an open censure: *You're a bad son for not visiting your mom.* The crescendo of guilt and shame triggered the angry part to scream, "Shut up!"

Sudden silence.

Tomas glanced around. Every eye was on him. Pastor Warren, mouth agape, had stopped speaking mid-sentence. That was when Tomas realized he had loudly vocalized his angry part.

Oh, no! What did I do?

You've made everyone mad!

Just leave. Now!

The noise in Tomas's head—his other parts, mortified about what had just happened—snapped him out of his daze. When he heard a *clang!*, Tomas realized his legs had bolted from under him, toppling his chair.

He sprinted out of the room. Only one need occupied his attention: to vanish.

Tomas reentered the classroom after everyone left, thinking he would apologize to Pastor Warren. But when the pastor responded by suggesting God was healing Tomas through his class, Tomas's anger reemerged, telling the pastor to be quiet.

He apologized for this, too, even though it did not quell his anger one bit.

As the weeks dragged on, Tomas emailed the pastor. And again. Then, he met with the dean and complained about Pastor Warren's exaggerated use of *mom*. While sympathetic to Tomas's frustration, the dean refused to meddle with how Pastor Warren ran his class. Not getting any help from his external world evaporated Tomas's appetite. He ended up fasting, for days on end, simply because he had no desire for food.

The turning point came when Tomas addressed his parts—*Guys, is there more to the story behind your intense reaction against Pastor Warren?*—and waited for their response.

His parts rewarded his patience with a distant memory. A pastor from Tomas's youth had moralized about how the Bible required Tomas to honor both his parents *and* him, the heavy-handed pastor, by fulfilling all their wishes. Tomas's parts also reminded him about his abusive stepfather and how he derived perverse pleasure from using Scripture to provoke him. "You call yourself a Christian? The Bible says you have to obey me."

Realizing the many times authority figures manipulated Tomas's parts to subjection stretched his heart for them. It also helped him understand why he had felt so guilty for not fulfilling his mother's requests to visit her. This realization made him feel compassionate toward his parts.

As compassion flowed, Tomas felt lighter. His parts felt his love for them and decided to release some of their guilt. (Feeling lighter when working with your part often means it has spontaneously unburdened.) The additional work Tomas did with his sad and guilty parts proved instrumental in restoring his internal equilibrium. His appetite returned with a vengeance. Snickering, Tomas told me he now needs to lose twenty pounds.

He also realized he no longer felt incensed at Pastor Warren. The entire ordeal—from the moment his angry part got activated to when it finally relented—lasted three months.

OSTRACIZED IN THE INTERNAL SYSTEM

Have you had a tiff with someone, and when you tried to defend yourself the person pretended you were invisible? If you applied the same scenario but to an entire organization, it would be akin to the church's prevailing attitude concerning anger. Instead of understanding what gives rise to this emotion, Christians tend to suppress it: *Let's do what we can to avoid anger. Pretend it doesn't exist.*

Can you appreciate how hard angry parts have to strive to keep sloshing on, despite this constant opposition?

But there is another—and more personal—reason life is difficult for our angry parts. Scripture says, "Wrath is cruel, anger is overwhelming" (Proverbs 27:4 ESV). This overwhelm is not only felt in the person's internal system, it also motivates parts to do everything they can to avoid any scenario that might induce future overwhelm. If you have battled a panic attack or witnessed one, for instance, you have firsthand experience of how unpleasant it is to be flooded with emotion. All this to say, when emotional overwhelm occurs because of anger, other parts can blame angry parts—which is why they are commonly abhorred by protector parts and feared by exiles.

Wendy, 43, has spent most of her life avoiding anger. Her protector parts argued anger did not fit her sunny disposition. Neither was there an acceptable place within her Asian culture to accommodate anger. These parts kept Wendy's rage at bay by rationalizing it away: *Your brother didn't mean to upset you. He's just eccentric.* They quoted verses about how anger was for fools

(Ecclesiastes 7:9). They minimized the infractions she noticed by shouldering the responsibility herself; somehow, they always traced the slights she felt back to her own fault.

When Wendy did IFS therapy, she sensed something lurking in the shadows of her mind. She became curious. *Who is it? Is it one of my parts? Why does it live in the dark?* Wendy's curiosity opened the door for the shadowy part to step forward.

As it emerged, Wendy saw it was her angry part, ready to tell Wendy more about itself. But Wendy felt hesitant. She wanted to know why this hesitancy developed, so she asked her internal system, *Who doesn't want me to listen to my angry part?*

The parts that had been confining Wendy's angry part responded, *It's a bad idea for you to befriend this part, when we've had to suppress it all along.* These protector parts pulled their ace card: there was a young part living in Wendy's heart, who remembered—and still trembled at—her father's anger.

She asked her parts to explain why they brought up the terrified young part in her heart. They answered, *Dad's anger terrorized the young part from the outside. Why would you let your own anger out, when doing that could frighten the young part from the inside?*

WHY ANGER EXISTS

Wendy's protectors exerted a valiant effort to restrain her anger. I commended them for their noble intention. At the same time, I explained to them how nobody can drive with green lights all the way; everyone everywhere encounters red lights some of the time.

I employed the traffic light analogy because, like red traffic lights that boldly command eighteen-wheelers to stop in their tracks, angry parts have no qualms about expressing themselves. They carry huge reservoirs of energy because it is their job to defend us when we suffer an injustice or when something stops us from our objective.[2] They are like the strong man in Jesus' parable: "How can anyone enter a strong man's house and carry off his possessions unless he first ties up the strong man? Then he can plunder his house" (Matthew 12:29). Angry parts are militant because they play a pivotal role.

Consider angry parts as guards who protect the valuables within our house—or, in this case, our heart. The more vulnerability that hides within, the more aggressive our angry parts will be. This universal principle applies whether or not we express our anger. As long as there are emotional wounds that are liable to get reinjured because of an external event, anger will arise to protect those tender parts.

However, if we consistently help our vulnerable parts, and if we keep unburdening them from past hurt, there will come a time when our angry part may decide to retire from its job. This principle works for Tomas, Wendy, me—and it will work for you too.

ANTI-ANGER VERSES: ANOTHER INTERPRETATION

Does Ephesians 4:31 sound like God is commanding us to abolish all anger? Read it slowly: "Get rid of all bitterness, rage and anger, brawling and slander, along with every form of malice." If you teeter on answering in the affirmative, hold that thought. This answer cannot offer us the full picture because a few verses earlier, in Ephesians 4:26, God designates sunset as anger's expiration time. Which means he is *not* instructing us to annihilate anger altogether.

To discover this verse's hidden message, scrutinize the order of the six nouns listed there. The verse starts off with *bitterness, rage, anger,* followed by *brawling, slander, malice.* The latter lot implies the presence of another person—because, as any married couple can attest, it takes two to brawl. Nobody slanders or commits malice against themselves. By drawing on this insight, we can interpret the verse as such: "If you let anger occupy a permanent place in your life, it will ransack your relationships."

When we apply this same understanding to other verses about anger, we get a friendly warning to *not* let anger color our regular response. So let's lean in, get to know our angry parts, find the hurt they are guarding, and heal said hurt. This way we can free angry parts from their burdens.

Remember Kermit's song? It started with a complaint about his skin color. By the time the song ended, however, he had had a change of heart. He had developed more love for himself. Likewise, it is possible for your angry part to relinquish its burdens and relish its life.

ANGER AT GOD

If you prayed hard but your childhood friend's baby died anyway, or your husband's business still folded, or some other unwanted turn of events happened, I can understand why your angry part would blame God. Or perhaps your animosity against the Almighty had been silently building over time, but when your younger brother perished in a hurricane—despite his passion for ministry—you hit the boiling point.

You are not alone in resenting God.

Psychologist Julie Exline has been studying anger issues for more than a decade and discovered that up to two-thirds of Americans harbor anger at God. Some were miffed because they did not get what they wanted. Others suffered (say, because of cancer) and blamed God for it.[3]

It is okay to have angry feelings about your loss. It is likewise okay to express them to God. But if you wish to hear his side of the story—like why he would let you go through such a terrible experience—keep an open channel of communication with the Almighty.

This does not mean you can only approach God after sanitizing yourself from anger. It *does* mean holding curiosity about God's response to your anger, even if some parts of you are convinced they already know what he would say. If you keep asking God, you will receive an answer. His own Son, Jesus, told us so (Matthew 7:7-8).

Maintaining a relationship with God is beneficial. We know this not just from the Bible, but also from a major survey. In 2020, Gallup polled 1,008 Americans and collected a surprise: despite the rise of the Covid-19 illness, those who attended weekly religious services rated their mental health as *better* than the year before.[4] If drawing closer to God improved mental health during the crazy Covid-19 pandemic era, then doing so while grieving must also do us good.

At least this was my experience. Without the Lord, I would not have had the wherewithal to weather my father's premature passing. Back when my father had just died, I bombarded heaven with silent questions. *How could he have died so unexpectedly? If I had prayed more, could I have averted this tragedy? Why didn't you alert me he was going to die? I didn't even have any time to pray for him!*

Slowly, over time, God answered. He showed me how he, in fact, sounded two warning bells. I heard the first as we rang in 2018. That is, I sensed something big was brewing, although I assumed it was going to be thrilling. *Maybe we'll finally get our dream house!* Unfortunately, even though the sensation I picked up from God was accurate—something big *was* happening—I neglected to seek him for details.

The second one sounded more like a thud. A few days after he returned home from his final trip to America, Papa suddenly lost consciousness and fell. Only later did we realize how weak his heart must have been at the time. It probably stopped pumping blood, at least momentarily, which caused him to faint.

After the incident, our entire family pleaded with him to schedule a checkup. But this was his last text to me: "I'd like to have a checkup. But it doesn't seem that serious."

He died a week later.

REASSURING RELUCTANT PARTS ABOUT ANGER

God does not play favorites (Romans 2:11). What he has done for me, he can do for you. Whatever consolation you need from God is yours for the taking—presuming you let him in, including into your rage-tinted grief.

Still, I can understand if you sense a reluctance to acknowledge your anger, and especially if it is aimed at God. How about if you tell your hesitant parts the following?

Allowing your angry part to explain its frustration will *not* offend God. Have you considered how, despite his omniscience about your anger, the Almighty has chosen *not* to obliterate you? As Nahum 1:3 assures us, God is slow to anger. But even if our anger somehow provokes him, "[God's] anger lasts only a moment, but his favor lasts a lifetime" (Psalm 30:5). His mercy never expires (Lamentations 3:22 ESV). He regards us with compassionate eyes, irrespective of our stance toward him.

If you are still skeptical, perhaps Moses' mistake in chapter one can help. We saw how God instructed him to speak to a rock. Moses struck it instead—twice—before taking credit for the miracle: "Water gushed out, and the community and their livestock drank" (Numbers 20:11).

Did you catch the significance of the story? Moses mishandled the situation and, as a result, forfeited his destiny. His action angered God. Yet the rock sprang forth fresh water anyway.

I would have thought Moses' mistake would have kept the miracle from manifesting. Is not obedience a prerequisite for divine plans to unfold? The same group of complaining Israelites missed their God-given opportunity to conquer the Promised Land because of disobedience (Hebrews 3:6–4:7). Since Moses disobeyed God, how could the miracle still happen?

Because God was merciful. Even though Moses disregarded his instruction, the people—and their animals—still required hydration.

Since mercy always triumphs over judgment (James 2:13), God provided a miracle to quench their thirst, despite Moses' misstep.

So let's return to any concerned parts you might have. Let them know it takes a tremendous amount of energy to repress anger. (Imagine how exhausting it would be if you were to force a lid over a boiling pot of water for hours.) Meanwhile, grieving zaps energy. But if you liberate anger from its restraints, you can harvest the energy you once used to repress this powerhouse to fuel the remainder of your grief journey instead.

If you still sense a reluctance to process your anger with God, tell your concerned parts one more thing. Listening to your angry part does not mean you will be overtaken by its rage. Your Self is capable to listen to any part, including the angry one, without building your life only on one part's perspective.

Any parts that are concerned about letting you meet the angry part are welcome to watch from the sidelines once the angry part shows up. It can also help to create a room in your soul that is both soundproof and feelings-proof.[5] A safe place, if you will. Then, you can invite parts that are concerned about the angry part to wait in this safe place until you are done with your angry part.

DIPPING INSIDE

Let's take what you read in this chapter and apply what is relevant.

With your other parts' permission, ask your angry part to show up without overwhelming you. (Place the angry part in a locked room if this makes other parts feel safer.)

Now, focus on the angry part. How are you noticing it? Write down its shape, thoughts, feelings, or the part's effect on you—for instance, perhaps you are feeling more irritated now than a moment ago.

_____

_____

_____

_____

If your angry part is flashing one frustrating memory after another, intensifying your emotion, ask it to slow down. Explain how you can hear it better if it does not overwhelm you.

_____

_____

_____

_____

Once your part slows down, ask yourself:

- *How do I feel toward my angry part?*
- *Do I have any curiosity about why it is enraged?*
- *Do I have compassion for how hard it must be for the part to store all this anger?* (If you have no curiosity or compassion, another part might be nearby. Ask any such parts to step back so you can remain open-hearted with the angry part.)

Keep asking yourself how you feel toward the angry part until you sincerely feel an openness toward it. Then, share your openness with the part.

_____

_____

_____

_____

How does the angry part respond?

_____

_____

_____

_____

Ask your part how it feels about itself. Does it lead a hard life, like its job, feel understood? Is there anything other than being angry that it would rather do? Note everything your part says.

_____

_____

_____

_____

Now, ask the part, *Why do you respond with anger regarding my loss? And who are you angry at?* Listen for what the part has to say.

_____

_____

_____

_____

What is your reaction as you hear everything the angry part has explained? Share it with the part and notice how it responds.

_____

_____

_____

_____

Ask the part, *Is there more you want to share, whether about the loss, why you respond in anger, or anything else?* Listen for more stories or memories from this part and record them here.

_____

_____

_____

Keep listening to your part so long as your heart is open to it. Taking a break is also okay. But please return to the angry part when you are ready to listen to it some more. Write everything you hear from the part.

_____

_____

_____

If the part has nothing else to share, ask, *Do you feel I have fully understood you?* If it confirms it—one way or another—ask if it is interested in releasing any of its anger. Once the part unburdens, you might feel lighter or less sullen.

_____

_____

_____

If your part is not ready to unburden, ask it, *What needs to happen first before you can unburden?* One possibility includes wanting to spend time with you without being placed in a locked room. Or perhaps it needs you to work with other parts first, like Tomas did with his sad and guilty parts.

But maybe your part needs to know why God allowed this horrible loss to happen. For God to show up, we need to approach him with all our heart (Jeremiah 29:13). One way to meet this condition is to create an openness inside, by asking parts for space. Therefore, ask the angry part, *Would you give me space as I talk to God? I promise to accurately represent you.*

If your part agrees, you will feel more spacious inside.

Then, invite God the Father, Lord Jesus Christ, or the Holy Spirit to join you. God's presence is sweet and gentle. The opposite of pushy. Once you sense the Lord, relay your part's heartaches or questions to him and wait for his response.

Do not be alarmed if there is no immediate reply. The Lord might answer you when you sleep, through someone else, when you browse through the Bible, or through some other ways at a later time. Keep an open heart as you expect his response.

Once this happens, you *will* know. His answer will not just satisfy your heart's quest, it will also click—like a missing puzzle piece, sitting snugly in its uniquely shaped space.

After you receive the divine response you were yearning for, schedule another visit with your angry part. Please also listen to its feedback about your conversation with God. If it has follow-up questions, convey them to God, and update your part on the answer. Keep going until you, and your part, are both satisfied.

Finally, thank it for talking with you. Thank all the other parts also—that is, every part that cleared the way so the angry part could meet with you.

11

Guilt and Regret

I KILLED MY BELOVED

"IF I WERE A BETTER DAUGHTER, Mother wouldn't have died."

That was what a part of Selena, 29, said. This part holds remorse about the aneurysm that killed her mother years ago, back when Selena was still a young teenager.

In contrast to the loss of her mother, Selena never missed her father, who abandoned the family when she was a baby. To compensate for his absence, her mother doused Selena with double the love. She worked multiple jobs so little Selena could carry a backpack filled with new notebooks and sharpened pencils at the beginning of each school year. Selena always received two birthday presents and two Christmas gifts every year.

Mother's death shut the door on Selena's contented childhood. Since there were no relatives to claim her, Selena became a ward of the state. She hopped from one foster family to the next until she turned eighteen. Afterward, Selena made a living by waitressing and working overtime hours while attending college part-time.

Selena had already disclosed her background prior to this session. But her claim about her culpability regarding her mother's death surprised me. "What do you mean, Selena?"

"I used to tease Mother about inviting one thousand people for my wedding. I also wanted to become a neurosurgeon. But since I was also interested in researching the brain, I told Mother I'd finish college and get a dual MD/PhD degree. Maybe thinking about my aspirations stressed her out. Maybe she didn't know how she was going to pay for these things and the stress hiked her blood pressure and triggered the aneurysm."

Selena concluded, "I killed my mother."

MULTIPLE ROADS TO GUILT

Guilt is a common reaction in bereavement. Survivor's guilt is especially potent if your loved one died from suicide. Rita Schulte, a grief counselor whose depressed husband shot himself in their bed, could not escape the responsibility she felt for his demise. "I should have forced Mike to get help sooner. I should have come back with him that day on the airplane . . . I should have been more reassuring on the phone the night before. I should have had him committed. I should have, I should have, I should have. In my mind, I was as guilty as if I had pulled the trigger for him."[1]

If you cared for your elderly father who then died, you may feel responsible. *If only I had obtained a second opinion, rushed him to the hospital sooner, insisted on another test,* a million other if-onlys. You may regret your decision to step out of your mother's hospital room because she died while you were away. Alternatively, your remorse may have to do with your culpability—a mistake you made when the person was still alive. Maybe you did not spend enough attention on your loved one. Or got into a thorny disagreement. Or decided to excommunicate the individual altogether.

It was early Saturday morning when Letty's cat, Comet, mewled nonstop. Still sleepy, she interpreted Comet's cries as a plea to go outside. Because Comet was used to coming in and out of the house, Letty thought nothing of letting her cat dart out the door so she could reclaim her sleep.

Except Comet never returned.

As the days passed by, rumors of a coyote sighting in the neighborhood struck Letty with tremendous guilt. When she opened the door for Comet, she also ushered him to his death! Her guilt intensified when she realized that, under pressure at work as an ad executive, she had neglected to refresh Comet's water bowl as frequently as before. She now realized how, given how hot the weather had been, Comet was likely pleading for more water that final morning. If she had refilled his water instead of letting him out, Comet's life might have been spared.

Letty knew there was a good chance he was no longer earthbound. Still, she pictured him in her mind's eye—and asked for his forgiveness. She felt her cat not only forgave her, but also thanked her for the love she had shown him throughout the years.

Regardless of how your guilt originated, let's follow Letty's lead and help your parts unburden. Grief researchers have found excessive guilt to be corrosive—affecting both physical and psychological health.[2] No wonder J. William Worden, in his book *Grief Counseling and Grief Therapy*, labeled guilt as one of the most problematic feelings for the bereaved.[3]

DIRECT FROM THE SOURCE

When Rita Schulte—the counselor whose husband shot himself—discovered an intake form he filled out at a treatment center, her guilt loosened. Mike had written wonderful things about her, which made her feel as though he could see how much she tried to help. Still, this realization only eased, not eliminated, her guilt.

The turning point in her healing came when Schulte saw her dead husband in her mind's eye.[4] When her therapist hooked her up to a bilateral brain stimulation machine, Schulte "saw" Mike. He told her the suicide was not her fault.

I am not trained in EMDR, the type of therapy Schulte chose, nor do I own a machine she utilized. (EMDR, or Eye Movement Desensitization and Reprocessing, is one of the most effective therapy approaches to heal psychological trauma.) But my experience in facilitating IFS mirrors hers. Some guilt-ridden parts may only feel relieved if they have an emotional experience with the deceased, like what happened with Schulte and her late husband. We could try and provide soothing and even reassuring remarks about how the loss was *not* our parts' fault, but this gesture alone often falls short. These parts may need to hear an absolution of sorts before they are ready to unburden.

RELEASING SELENA'S GUILT

Selena, from the beginning of the chapter, is an example of this. Selena's guilty part insisted she was culpable for her mother's premature death. Despite her logical part's analysis for why such a belief was irrational, and even with Selena's vigorous rebuttal, the guilty part persisted: "Was her life with me so terrible that Mother had to escape it? Why didn't she take better care of herself?" Because nothing else satisfied the part, I wondered if Selena's part might benefit from hearing Mother's answer.

My inquiry wrinkled Selena's forehead. This devout Christian felt guarded about the idea, for fear of breaking God's rule. She took some time off-session to pray and ponder. Should she proceed with the exercise?

The next session began with Selena's ingenious solution. "Is it okay to invite Jesus? That way I can convey my questions to him and he can relay them to Mother. I don't think I'll violate any scriptural mandate this way."

"Perfect," I replied. "Let's find the guilty part first. Then we'll invite Jesus."

Selena had been doing IFS for a few years, which meant she knew how to focus inward to connect with her guilty part. The part soon showed up—loaded with feelings of remorse and low self-esteem. Selena greeted her part with compassion and invited Jesus into the session. Then she invited her part to express its questions about Mother's death.

Her voice quivering, Selena voiced her part's question. "Jesus, did my mother feel she had to die to escape life with me? Please ask her for me."

Her inquiry blurred my eyes as twin streams slid down Selena's face. She later reported seeing tears pooling in the Lord's eyes too.

After a period of silence, Selena reported how she sensed the Lord informing her of the following: "Your mom felt she was doing her best, given the baggage she inherited from previous generations. She didn't want to leave. More specifically, she didn't want to leave *you*." Selena felt extra touched because Jesus emphasized the last word.

This session informed Selena's guilty part that her mother had faced pressures that preceded her existence. This revelation freed the part from its guilt.

DIPPING INSIDE

You may have one part that holds both guilt and regret simultaneously. Alternatively, you may have parts that feel guilty while other parts feel mostly regret. Either way, ask the parts who feel guilty and regretful to show up and assess how many part(s) show up.

_____

_____

_____

Do you feel compassionate or curious toward these parts? If you
do not, there might be other parts that feel hesitant to let you
access the guilty or remorseful parts. What is their concern?
Assure them that listening to these parts does not mean you will
be flooded with remorse.

_____

_____

_____

_____

Check again. Do you feel compassionate or curious toward the
remorseful parts now? If so, please share that sentiment with
your parts.

How do they respond?

_____

_____

_____

_____

If you are not sensing anything, ask your internal world, *Is another part blocking me? Please explain so I can better understand you.*
See if you can broker an agreement so you can be alone with the
guilty/regretful parts. Keep going until you feel a stronger connection with the target part(s).

Once you establish this connection, check again if the same compassion or curiosity is around. If so, send it to the parts and notice their response.

_____

_____

_____

_____

Let your parts know you are here for them. Ask, *What do you want me to know about you?* In addition, you can also ask your parts any of the following:

- *How do you feel regarding my loss?*

- *Do you tend to feel guilty in general?*

- *What do you regret about this situation?*

- *What happened that caused you to feel guilty the first time? Did someone shame or blame you?*

Write down your parts' response.

_____

_____

_____

_____

Can you understand why they feel regretful or guilty? Then let them know.

_____

_____

_____

_____

Are your parts interested in hearing God's view about whether they are justified in their guilt and regret? If this question provokes fear, assure your parts that God is good. (As one author commented, "Goodness looks like God."[5]) The One who commanded us to speak the truth in love (Ephesians 4:15) will not violate his own edict. Even his corrections are draped with grace.

Listen to what the Lord says about your guilt and regret.

If God gently informed you that your guilt and regret are justified, let your parts know that forgiveness can unleash healing. Are they willing to ask forgiveness from the one they wronged? Once you sense a yes, help your parts apologize for their wrongdoing in the matter.

_____

_____

_____

_____

But if God told you your parts are holding on to unnecessary guilt and regret, ask your parts if they inherited those feelings from someone else. Listen to their story.

_____

_____

_____

_____

Are your parts willing to release their burden? Decide on how to destroy the collective burden: by burning it, shipping it to outer space, casting it to God (1 Peter 5:7), or something else.

How about asking God for a gift in lieu of the burden? Jot down what you sense the Lord wants to give your parts and simply receive them.

_____

_____

_____

_____

Ask if your parts have anything more to say or ask of you. Let them know you have noted their message or request. (Whatever promise you made to your parts, please follow through.)

_____

_____

_____

_____

If there is nothing else, warmly thank your parts for trusting you. Thank the other parts that made space for the guilty and remorseful parts as well.

12

Fear

MORE CONTAGIOUS THAN COVID-19

HER PARENTS' DECISION TO FLY despite the fog made an instant orphan out of Leigh. Her dad's enormous success as a trial lawyer meant her parents traveled frequently. An able team of domestic helpers—a live-in nanny, housekeeper, and two babysitters—supervised Leigh and her younger brothers whenever they were gone.

Leigh's parents were on their way home after a trip to the Maldives when their private plane crashed. In addition to losing her parents, Leigh also gained fear.

The tragedy struck long before her own two kids came into the picture, and still, Leigh confided, "The last time I spoke with my parents was before they got on the plane. Dad said they'd see us soon. Mom was going to show off her tan and the cute sundresses she bought. But we never saw them again. Now I'm afraid Adrian and the kids might also die suddenly. Life goes one way and you expect it'll continue to go that way until one day, it doesn't."

Do you resonate with Leigh's fear? The participants in Elyce Wakerman's study did. Wakerman's father died when she was a child, which prompted her to study the effects of father-lessness on daughters. She found that women who grew up in a fatherless household—whether because of death, divorce, or abandonment—feared their spouses were going to die.[1]

Fear of the unknown, of navigating the world without our deceased loved ones, is a common fear. For families impacted by suicide, surviving members often develop fear of their own self-destructive impulses.[2]

And then there is fear of losing the memories we have of the deceased. It was not that long ago that Papa left, and already my mind cannot recall his voice: *What other details am I losing?* my fearful part whispered. *I don't want to forget Papa!*

Both C. S. Lewis and Madeleine L'Engle had this same fear,[3] answered another part, attempting to console this one.

So what? retorted my fearful part. *That doesn't help one bit.*

I watched this internal back and forth with increasing worry: *What if memories of my father keep evaporating?* But then it dawned on me how half of my DNA are copies of his. The shape of my feet came straight from him. I showed my fearful part how my shoes were positioned by the door—forming a rough V—and how this posture was recreated every single time I removed my footwear. Exactly like him. *It's impossible to forget what's encoded in me. Therefore, there are things about my father I will never forget.*

Once this realization settled, my fearful part exhaled its stress.

Fear has tremendous potential to shape our responses and therefore, future. This is why helping parts that struggle with fear is crucial.

COVID-19 PANDEMIC

Prior to the pandemic, fear was commonplace. But Covid-19 catapulted it to another stratosphere. It was fear of contracting the coronavirus that drove the world to a literal lockdown. Nations implemented strict measures to curb the spread of the virus, including by mandating large gatherings—schools, houses of worship, and others—to disperse. Governing bodies around the globe shielded the most vulnerable among us, isolating the elderly and infirm.

Despite the positive intentions behind these regulations, some were injured in the process. Isolating those who were Covid-ridden meant some patients suffered and died without their loved ones' physical presence, which hurt both the sick *and* those who loved them. Ken Doka, an expert on grief, noted how "the company of others eases dying, but it also facilitates the subsequent grief of survivors."[4]

Covid-19 changed our world. This virus altered not just how we live—with working from home gaining global acceptance, for example—but also how we think. Listen to Doka's explanation about our mindset post-pandemic: "We no longer see the world as safe, predictable, or benevolent. . . . This adds another complicating layer to grief as the world now is experienced as more dangerous and unexpected than believed. Thus, we not only deal with the death of an individual but the loss of the world as once experienced, leading to increased anxiety and depression."[5]

Simply put, the virus unleashed more fear than ever. We responded by adapting to this increased level. Known as *habituation*, the phenomenon means we have grown so accustomed to fear, it will now take more of it to create a rise in us.[6]

Not good. Especially given the Bible's repeated admonition against fear:

> Be strong and courageous. Do not be afraid or terrified because of them, for the LORD your God goes with you; he will never leave you nor forsake you. (Deuteronomy 31:6)

Say to those with fearful hearts, "Be strong, do not fear; your God will come, he will come with vengeance; with divine retribution he will come to save you." (Isaiah 35:4)

Do not fear, for I am with you; do not be dismayed, for I am your God. I will strengthen you and help you; I will uphold you with my righteous right hand. (Isaiah 41:10)

Therefore do not worry about tomorrow, for tomorrow will worry about itself. Each day has enough trouble of its own. (Matthew 6:34)

Peace I leave with you; my peace I give you. I do not give to you as the world gives. Do not let your hearts be troubled and do not be afraid. (John 14:27)

God gave his Word for our sake: "Keep my commands, and you will live" (Proverbs 4:4). Following his directions, including to stop being afraid, will serve us well. Besides, God dwells inside us through his Spirit (John 14:16-17). He fights for us, comforts us, meets all our needs, and then some (Deuteronomy 1:30; 3:22; Psalm 56:9; 68:20; 119:50, 76; Philippians 4:19).

So why do we—Christians included—live fearfully?

FEAR-PROOFING YOUR LIFE

One answer is that we do not know how to execute God's command. Consider the following verse: "Remove grief and anger from your heart and put away pain from your body, because childhood and the prime of life are fleeting" (Ecclesiastes 11:10 NASB 1995). Some might interpret this verse as a rallying call to quash both grief and anger. But if so, we have a serious problem; when we avoid negative feelings, we are also amplifying them over time.[7]

If you wish to liberate your heart from grief—or anger—on a permanent basis, you need to uproot the reason for their existence. The same is true about fear.

Truth is, God will not forcefully remove anything our parts are unwilling to forgo. He is not a cruel dictator who badgers us into subjugation with brute power. This is why praying for God to eliminate your fear may only foster temporary relief—because as long as there is a part of us that clings to fear, it will wedge open a back door for fear to worm its way back into our internal world.

A more effective approach, as you will soon see, is to befriend your fearful part first. "Your fears are probably the single best map of what you actually value," write J. Alasdair Grove and Winston T. Smith in *Untangling Emotions*.[8] Only by getting to know your fearful part will you learn what this part values and why it is so afraid. The act of befriending this part will help it relinquish its fear—in time.

RESOLVING LEIGH'S FEAR

Since Leigh's parents died in a plane accident, she has been harboring fear of her own family's premature death. So I asked her, "How do you feel toward the part with this fear?"

"My heart goes out to it," she responded.

"Please share your compassion with it."

Leigh closed her eyes and silently worked with her part inside. After a few minutes passed by, her eyes misted. "The part feels grateful I'm willing to hear it out. It says I'm usually so busy with the kids and never have time for myself."

"How do you feel about what your part said?"

"A little guilty. My part is right. I often neglect myself."

"I get how there would be a part of you that feels guilty about not spending enough time with your own internal system. But would that guilty part be willing to give you some space to be with the fearful part?" I had to ask Leigh to create this internal space. Our target part is the fearful part, not the one with the guilty feelings.

"Oh, I didn't even realize there's another part. Let me ask the guilty part to relax." Leigh went silent before returning with a report. "Okay, the guilty part is stepping back."

"Great. If you haven't, please thank that part before focusing on the fearful part again."

Leigh nodded.

"Is the fearful part still there? How are you noticing this one?"

"I feel fear radiating from my torso. The fear is that something bad will happen to the kids and Adrian. This part looks like me when I was a teenager. She can't help but replay all the possible scenarios that could take my family out."

"Are you okay with this amount of fear? If it doesn't overwhelm you, let's continue."

"I'm fine. And I feel for her."

"Let the part feel your compassion. What does she need to heal?"

"She needs to say goodbye to my parents. Their deaths shook her. So the part wanted to go back to before the accident so she could better prepare. I think it's a good idea."

When we offer do-overs to parts, we do *not* change historical facts. What happened still happened. But a do-over creates the opportunity for your Self to be with the target part the way nobody was there for it before. Do-overs help parts feel supported, which often encourages them to release their burden. Also, according to Frank Anderson, the do-over step in the IFS protocol can rewire our nervous system. When Self provides a corrective emotional experience for an exile, the neural network concerning the memory of the unpleasant incident is accessed, updated, and rewired.[9]

I told Leigh, "Let's ask the part to take us back in time and direct the do-over."

Leigh closed her eyes and stayed silent. When she emerged, she shared with me what transpired internally. "My part and I went to what looked like a condominium my parents must have rented in the Maldives. It overlooked the ocean with a large patio in front. They were standing there, gazing at the clear water, when I walked in. Mom looked surprised but happy to see me. Dad's favorite beverage was bourbon and sure enough, he had a tumbler in his hand. My part and I greeted him and asked him to pour me one. He said, 'But you don't drink.' I told him, 'I do for special occasions, now that I'm an adult.' Then my part told him, point blank, 'You'll die today,' and although Dad seemed surprised, he didn't object. Then my part invited my brothers and our friends to come. We had a fabulous party, complete with a band and catered food. But after a while my part looked at my parents and said, 'It's time.' I hugged them both—"

Leigh paused and inhaled deeply.

"—and first my mom, then my dad went inside and climbed the stairs. They waved at us. I'm sure in real life the stairs went to one or at most two upper stories, but I saw my parents kept going up and up and up. Meanwhile, the partygoers told my part how cool my parents were. They chanted my parents' names over and over."

By the time she finished telling me what happened internally, sobs had shaken Leigh's shoulders. Tears fell freely from her face. A mixture of pride and compassion welled up in me—not just because Leigh and her part did a transformative do-over, but also for the agony of losing her parents at a young age.

While Leigh reached for tissues, I asked if her fearful part was willing to release its burden regarding her parents' premature death.

"Yes," Leigh answered. "My part's burden looked like sandbags she hid under her shirt. They held the fear that Adrian and the kids would die young. She released those sandbags into the ocean."

Leigh then reported seeing her teenage part sunning on a pristine, white beach, sipping an Arnold Palmer. The part invited courage to face the future to replace the fear.

UNATTACHED BURDENS

The apostle Paul wrote, "God gave us a spirit not of fear but of power and love and self-control" (2 Timothy 1:7 ESV). This, in addition to other well-known verses against fear, compel some in the church to treat fear exclusively through spiritual means. Accordingly, certain segments of the church practice deliverance ministry—akin to what Jesus did in the Gospels. (For example, see Matthew 8:16; Mark 1:34, 39; Mark 16:9; Luke 4:31-35.)

Can spiritual factors propagate fear? Definitely. In the Bible, these culprits are referred to as unclean, evil, or impure spirits (Matthew 12:43). Around the IFS community they are known as Unattached Burdens (UBs). The most important thing to know about these invisible entities is sometimes they penetrate our internal systems without permission.

Different UBs drag with them different odious baggage. I found a UB that misled the host person to believe she brought on her terminal illness diagnosis by having too good of a life. One UB made the person feel guilty for bucking the family's rigid expectations. Other UBs push the host person to self-sabotage, to always sacrifice for everyone else's benefit, to doubt God's power, and yes, to be fearful.

The next time you sense any degree of dread, therefore, pause and ask, *Where is this fear coming from?* Ask your parts if they have any knowledge about whether there is a UB in your system. In my experience, whenever there is a UB, parts will raise a stink. For instance, your parts might insist this thing is not "one of us."

When in doubt, ask the Holy Spirit. Because the Holy Spirit lives within you (1 Corinthians 3:16) and never lies (John 16:13), he *will* tell you if a UB has snuck into your inner world.

If you did find a UB, feel free to expel it. The process is similar to evicting a squatter from your property. You have the same authority over your mental residence as you do your physical one. Use Jesus' name to expel this invisible intruder (Philippians 2:10).

Then, seal your system with Jesus' blood so the UB cannot wreak more havoc (Matthew 12:43-45).

Check your fear level afterwards. If you do not sense any fear, then what you feared previously was likely caused by the UB. Double-check with your parts and see if they need your comfort or assurance after the UB leaves.

DIPPING INSIDE

But what if you expel the UB and there is still fear inside? This might indicate the presence of a part within you who is fearful. Just as parts can feel confused or conflicted, it is possible for them to feel afraid.

Let's start by preparing yourself to look inward, as we did in chapter two. When you are ready, use the following prompts to get to know your fearful part.

PROMPTS FOR YOUR PARTS

Ask your internal system for permission to meet the fearful part.

If you are encountering resistance—for instance, because you feel intimidated by the thought of meeting a fearful part—you might be blended with another part. Ask the intimidated part to open up space so you do not feel so apprehensive. If nothing changes, ask the part, *What are you afraid of?* If the answer is somewhere along the lines of not feeling confident you can go through this exercise successfully, let the part know this conclusion is premature. We will never know unless we try, so ask your part, *Will you give me a chance to go through the steps? You can stand back and watch as I continue my inward journey.*

But maybe the part is not concerned about that. It could be the fear has more to do with overwhelm—that if you meet your fearful parts, its fear might flood you. If so, let the part know you can ask the fearful part *not* to overwhelm you.

Keep working with any hesitant part until you sense a green light to find the fearful part. (You can tell this hesitant part has given you space if you feel more peaceful inside.)

Once you sense the fearful part coming forward, ask yourself, *How am I noticing it?* Jot it here. One reliable sign is if you feel an increase in fear. With a name like that—*fearful*—it makes sense if its presence reeks of fear.

What would you do if you came across a terrified, trembling little girl? My guess is you would not scold her for being a 'fraidy cat. You might squat down to her eye level instead. If you inquire what evoked such terror in her, I imagine you would do so with a soft tone and gentle gaze.

Keep this visual in mind as you get to know your fearful part. Your part may or may not look like that shuddering girl, but I guarantee it would appreciate your patience and kindness. Use these questions to prime your conversation with the part and write down the answers.

How old are you?

_____

_____

_____

Do you know me? Or my current age? (Often, our parts know only
the younger version of us. Updating parts with our current age
frequently helps them relax.)

_____

_____

_____

_____

What are you afraid of?

_____

_____

_____

_____

When did you start feeling afraid?

_____

_____

_____

_____

What do you need before you can release this fear?

_____

_____

Ask the part, *Is there anything else you would like to share with me about your fear?* Note its answers here. Please keep tuning into your part until it does not have anything else to share with you.

Let your part feel your sincerity and compassion. Do you understand why it feels afraid? Please share it with your part. Then, check if the part feels heard and seen by you.

My Christian clients seek the Lord's support when their part struggles with fear, because whenever Jesus arrives at the scene, his presence defuses fear. There is a reason he is called the Prince of Peace (Isaiah 9:6). When we invite Jesus, his presence comes with perfect love, which will then cast out all fear (1 John 4:18).

But you do not have to be a saint to invite Jesus into your internal world. He loves you regardless of your religious affiliation or how you have lived your life. The Bible says, "Everyone who calls on the name of the Lord will be saved" (Romans 10:13). The Greek word for "save," *sozo*, means more than just the spiritual act of entering heaven upon death. It also means to save those suffering on the earth, including by healing and making them well.[10]

Whoever you are, you are welcome to ask Jesus to heal you. He will not reject you.

If you wish to invite Jesus into your internal dialogue, let's do so now. You can discern his presence by a few telltale signs.

A pleasant memory from Sunday school or church might come unbidden. Maybe you are becoming aware of a snippet of a comforting verse. Or you might "hear" a portion of a hymn or worship song. You might also "see" a man you *know* is Jesus.

One thing is certain, God does *not* terrorize us. How can he, when he is gentleness personified? You can sense his heart for you and instinctively know he is telling you the truth. (These characteristics of God are from Psalm 16:11; Hosea 11:9 NKJV; John 1:14; 16:13; Galatians 5:22-23.)

Give Jesus time to do what he needs to heal your part.

_____

_____

_____

_____

You can also ask him, "Jesus, what do you want to say to me or my part—particularly about its fear?" Ask Jesus to explain why your part does not have to fear a single thing.

After Jesus supplies the answer, check with your part. How does it feel about Jesus' personal message for it?

_____

_____

_____

_____

When parts feel understood, they are often ripe for unburdening. Check with your part if it feels you have fully understood its position. Does it feel your support? Is it ready to release its fear?

If the answer is yes, wonderful. Ask how the part would like to give up its fear. If Jesus is still there, the part can hand off any fear that was previously stored in its body, mind, or emotions to Jesus. He knows what to do with fear.

But if your part is reluctant to let go, find out why. Ask your part, *Is there a reason you prefer to keep this fear?*

You can also ask your part if it is interested in a gradual release. That is, the part can choose to release a portion of its fear and see how it feels afterwards. If it does not like the aftermath of unburdening, the part can take up its fear again.

Keep leaning into the process until your part has no more fear.

_____

_____

_____

_____

If your part releases its fear, ask, *Would you like to invite any positive qualities to replace this fear?* Invite these qualities into your system.

_____

_____

_____

_____

Check in with your part on a regular basis in the next three to four weeks. This is a good practice after each unburdening.

Before you close your internal session, thank the part for working with you, as well as all other parts that made space for this fearful part.

See how half of my DNA are copies of my father's? (Honolulu, Hawaii)

Loneliness and Isolation

STEPS AWAY FROM DEATH

MEET STACIE, A WOMAN who sought IFS therapy a week after she turned 36. After her prematurely born baby did not make it, Stacie refused to leave home. With her blinds tightly drawn and no lights on, she might as well have hung a Do Not Disturb sign on life. Stacie only called my office after her best friend found my information and insisted that Stacie follow up.

Her desire for motherhood was birthed as her singleness refused to die. Year after year, Stacie saw peers and coworkers coupling up, finding their significant others one after another. So when her bestie also found her happily ever after, Stacie decided to give dating apps a try; however, for every decent date she found, she had to endure ninety-nine questionable others. The ridiculous ratio exhausted her into deleting her online profile. But it also highlighted how alone she was.

Stacie's disastrous love life convinced her to swap dates for diapers. So she pursued artificial insemination, hoping a baby would cure her loneliness.

Once she started therapy, Stacie's loneliness motivated her to keep coming back; at least she now had a therapist who would hear her out. However, when we attempted to access her lonely part, another part—her critic—intervened. (When you attempt to connect with an exile like loneliness, it is common for protector parts to show up first. In Stacie's case it was an inner critic. Whichever protectors block your access to your lonely part, negotiate with them with patience and confidence until they let you connect with your lonely part.)

"I heard this accusation in my head. *Nobody stays in bed all day. You're still stuck in the same rut and yet you call yourself an adult?*" Stacie reported.

It often helps to respond to critical parts directly, a technique known in IFS as Direct Access. I explained that all Stacie needed to do was to let her critic speak through her. After she gave me permission to proceed, I asked the critic, "Did you know Stacie has just lost her baby?"

No response.

I chose a different angle. "What do you mean, she's stuck in the same rut?"

This time Stacie's critic complained to me about Stacie: "She throws a pity party whenever something bad happens. She became depressed when her high school crush chose her best friend as his date for senior prom. She cried non-stop whenever a boyfriend cheated on her or broke up with her. She also moped around when she got fired from her first job. And now she deleted her dating profile. If she keeps isolating herself she'll never end up with anybody and wake up at 50, alone and maybe homeless!"

"Okay," I said, "so you want to protect Stacie from losing her job and from a life of permanent aloneness. But what if there's a better way to achieve your goal? For instance, by allowing Stacie to get to know the part of her that feels lonely?"

It took a while to assuage Stacie's inner critic. Even when it relented, other protector parts showed up, trying to convince Stacie (and me) how visiting the lonely region of her internal landscape was futile. Dangerous, even. What if Stacie became overwhelmed by all the losses she has sustained, worsening her depression?

"We can ask her exiles not to overwhelm Stacie," I assured her protectors. "Plus, if you allow Stacie to visit the lonely part, she can help the part feel less alone, which would make life a lot easier for you too."

Because Stacie kept her patience and persistence, these parts eventually allowed her to meet the young, lonely part. We will read about that session soon.

LONELINESS KILLS

In a *New Yorker* article, Tad Friend quoted a psychiatrist who had ample experience with those who vaulted to their deaths from the Golden Gate bridge. The doctor singled out a case that especially moved him: "The guy was in his thirties, lived alone, pretty bare apartment. He'd written a note and left it on his bureau. It said, 'I am going to walk to the bridge. If one person smiles at me on the way, I will not jump.'"[1]

But, sadly, he jumped, which must mean nobody smiled at him.

This touching story deserves our attention for so many reasons, including the vital importance of being kind to everyone (Ephesians 4:32) and caring for others' interests (Philippians 2:4). Who knows if our next smile can literally save a soul from suicide?

But there is one detail about his tragic story that made me wonder if loneliness often plagued this man. His apartment was "pretty bare," as though his external environment merely depicted what he felt inside.

Brené Brown, the popular social scientist and researcher, defined loneliness as an absence of meaningful social interaction.[2] A poverty of connections, if you will. Could it be this man was so devoid of human connections that it afflicted his soul with chronic loneliness, which then compelled him to choose death?

Hold that thought as I share about what Eric Marcus, a journalist, author, and podcaster, said about writers' deaths. In his book *Why Suicide?* Marcus exposes how writers have a high suicide rate. (Think Sylvia Plath, Virginia Woolf, Ernest Hemingway.) According to Marcus, an elevated risk of suicide in the writing community has to do with the "isolation that goes along with being a writer and how that contributes to bleak thoughts."[3] There they are, the same risk factors, turning up again. Chronic loneliness. Isolation. Being alone all the time.

But perhaps Marcus' poignant observation only affects writers. Maybe being isolated can be fatal, but only for the writing community. Or does loneliness kill large swaths of people?

We have reasons to believe the latter. By the time I write this chapter, reports are emerging about the number of fatalities because of the Covid-19 pandemic and the ensuing lockdown. One statistic highlighted those who died not because of the coronavirus itself, but due to assisted suicide. "Recent research has shown that in a considerable percentage of euthanasia cases in the Netherlands, loneliness features as one of the aspects of their unbearable suffering, especially among those whose natural deaths are not reasonably foreseeable."[4]

This research was not based on a puny little number with small statistical power. Before publishing his finding, the researcher had reviewed 4,000 euthanasia reports.[5]

Loneliness and isolation were also the reason given by 13.7 percent of the Canadians who opted for euthanasia. A Belgium rest home director attributed loneliness (due to the lockdown) as the reason behind an unprecedented rise in requests for information on euthanasia.[6]

We can discuss more individual studies like these, but my impatient part urges me to cut to the chase. So let's scrutinize the result of a meta-analysis (or a study on multiple studies) on loneliness.

Take a guess. Which of the following carries the highest risk of dying early: air pollution, obesity, excessive drinking, or loneliness?

If you picked the last one, bingo. Whereas the first three add a 5 percent, 20 percent, and 30 percent risk of dying early, respectively, loneliness lays on a whopping 45 percent risk.[7] Who would have thought loneliness is more dangerous than alcohol abuse?

Chronic loneliness can lead to death. Scientific studies and anecdotal evidence—from the famous writers who killed themselves, to the man who jumped off the Golden Gate bridge—support this conclusion. Of course, not all lonely souls kill themselves, thank God. Still, research shows how destructive loneliness can be: it leaves us feeling depressed and compromises the well-being of both our brain and body.[8]

LESSENING LONELINESS

How can we lessen loneliness while mourning? Is it by surrounding ourselves with people?

Yes. Grief feels lighter when you can share yours with a sympathetic ear. So if you have not done it, find supportive people to prop you up. Volunteer. Socialize. Read a nourishing book for the kids at your local library. Attend church.

Then again, being around people can sound as charming as chewing raw garlic. As a child, my husband John fought off stubborn cold symptoms this way. His mother was right; the trick worked. But, as you can imagine, the experience was highly unpleasant to young John. Similarly, being around people can help, but when we are gripped with loneliness, it can make us laser-focused on the negative parts of socializing, causing us to skip the whole idea altogether.[9] No wonder Brené Brown said she often feels the loneliest when others are around.[10]

Then what? When parts of us compel us to hunker down and tune out the world, what can be done for our lonely parts?

We can befriend them.

BEFRIENDING LONELY PARTS

After Stacie's protectors allowed her to visit her lonely part, she scanned her body to see if she could detect the part's presence. When focusing on her torso, she reported how heavy her chest felt. "Like the tenseness you feel in your upper diaphragm before you ugly cry" is how Stacie described the sensation.

She continued, "The part is a younger version of me, curled up in my childhood bed. The room is dark. She's hearing my mom fight with her latest boyfriend. She wishes Mom would come into her room instead. She has stuffed animals and Barbies all around her because she's always alone. She's an only child and never has friends over."

"How old is this part?" I ask.

"About 6."

"How do you feel toward your part, Stacie?" I ask.

"Lots of compassion."

"Would you share your compassion with her?"

After connecting with her part internally, Stacie informed me, "The part was guarded. I could sense she's afraid of getting hurt. This part believes everyone, including me, will eventually leave her because she's unlovable."

"Please check if the part knows who you are."

Stacie shook her head. "No. That's why she suspected I'd hurt her, just like everyone else. But after I introduced my Self, she relaxed a little."

"That's wonderful. Now, do you understand what your part said about being unlovable? Or do you need this part to show you why she developed these beliefs?"

Stacie had an idea why her part felt strongly about this, but she wanted to hear more. So she asked the part to explain.

As she listened inwardly, Stacie recalled how shy she was as a child. She wetted her pants because she felt too intimidated to ask her teacher to use the restroom. She could not keep eye contact. Having an alcoholic mother with a rotating roster of boyfriends meant young Stacie was, for all practical purposes, neglected.

"There were days when all I did was skulked to school, talked to no one, hurried home, locked myself in my room and blasted the music to eliminate the loneliness. And it muffled my mom's shouts. Why can't people love me? What do I need to do to be accepted? I can't keep trying to figure out how to stop people from abandoning me."

"Stacie, how do you feel toward your part, now that you've heard these things?" I asked.

"I feel bad. Inside, I'm sitting next to my part and side-hugging her."

"How does your part respond?"

"She doesn't say anything, but her body language is less rigid." At this, Stacie dropped her shoulders.

"What would it be like for your lonely part if you could be the one accepting her?"

The corners of her mouth curled up. Stacie reported, "My part is nodding. She's willing to give it a try."

DIPPING INSIDE

Being around others can help mitigate loneliness. But it can also multiply your pain. That is why, to ease loneliness, the safest first step is to turn inward and offer your presence for your lonely part. This way the lonely part does not need to hunt for someone suitable in the external world to befriend. While not everyone is willing or able to help, the real you—your Self—is always available.

Besides, the more your lonely part trusts you, the more it will allow you to lead the way in case someone makes an insensitive comment. Your Self can handle relational ruptures in a firm but loving way.

If the idea of mingling with others turns you off, however, let's start our journey into your inner system using this entry point.

Healing whatever caused this part to block you from connecting with others will help further your grief journey.

PROMPTS FOR YOUR PARTS

Ask your inner system, *Is there any part that refuses to be around people?* If so, ask them to identify themselves in whatever way they choose—by showing up in your mind's eye, letting you hear their thoughts, causing a feeling or memory to arise, or creating a physical sensation. Wait until you sense a response from your internal system.

_____

_____

_____

_____

Once you sense a part responding, jot down how you notice this part. Does it have a shape, size, color, message? Where is this part in or around you?

_____

_____

_____

_____

How do you feel toward the part that wishes to be alone? If your answer excludes any of the 8 C's—flip back to chapter two for these—it means there is a part (or more) blended with you. Please ask the parts with these other feelings to give you space. Keep asking these parts to open up space with you until you are genuinely curious or compassionate toward the part that wants you to avoid people.

_____

_____

_____

_____

Ask the part, *Why don't you want me to be around others?* Listen with an open heart and write down the answer you hear.

_____

_____

_____

_____

Do you understand your part's answer? If not, ask it to elaborate.

_____

_____

_____

_____

Let's say the part told you something like *People can't be trusted*. Maybe the part displayed scenes of loved ones who betrayed or otherwise hurt you. If you understand this part's point, let it know. Then, let it know you can process this hurt with the part. (If the part agrees to do this with you, please follow through. Sit with your internal system and heal any hurt caused by being in connection with others—whether in a romantic context, with family, friends, or authority figures. Space limitations mean we cannot get into the how here. Look up videos other IFS professionals have posted online if you are unsure how to proceed. Better yet, find your own IFS therapist.)

Your presence can help alleviate loneliness in your system. Your Self knows how to befriend the lonely part. So, ask your system to allow the lonely part to meet with you. It is possible the first part we met earlier—the one resisting you from being around people—*is* the lonely part. As usual, if you are unsure, ask the part directly.

Once the part shows up, ask yourself how you feel toward the part. If the answer is compassionate, curious, or any of the other 8 C's, extend the feeling toward the part.

_____

_____

_____

_____

How does the part respond?

_____

_____

_____

_____

Ask the part if it knows you, including your current age. Does it see how you carry strength and confidence in your core? If it does not, introduce your Self by inviting your part to peek into your heart. What (or who) does it see there?

_____

_____

_____

_____

If your lonely part sees someone sturdy or loving, the part is seeing your Self. Check in with the part about its burden. Ask it to share with you—in a piecemeal fashion—what it has been carrying, especially regarding the loss you are mourning. Write down what you hear.

_____

_____

_____

_____

Pause if you need to before hearing more from this part. Doing so will keep you from feeling flooded.

_____

_____

_____

If you understand your part's plight, let your part know and check the impact of your validation. Does your part feel supported by your understanding?

_____

_____

_____

Lean into your part. Keep it up until it has told you everything.

_____

_____

_____

_____

Jesus already called you—and your part—his friend (John 15:15). Is the part interested in reciprocating his bid for connection? If so, ask Jesus to come. Let your part interact with him. As you would with any other friend, you can build a friendship with Jesus by lingering in his presence. You can also ask him questions and listen to his answers. Write down what you hear.

_____

_____

_____

_____

When the time feels right, ask your lonely part, *Does this help?* If the part agrees, ask another question: *Would you like to do this again?* Your part would likely feel less lonely if you continue to spend time with it on a regular basis. So if you hear a yes, set aside more time with this part. Invite Jesus again and again if your part is agreeable.

_____

_____

_____

_____

Finally, please thank your part for trusting you.

PART 4

The Future

Other Possible Parts

THE LETTER MAX RECEIVED was as succinct as it was cruel: "This notice is to inform you that your father has intentionally disinherited you."

What kind of a father would do that?

Apparently, an abusive one. Max's dad once slapped his face so many times, young Max had to skip school for two straight days; the bruises would have been too obvious to escape public scrutiny. Max and his siblings shared a routine of scattering to their rooms whenever they heard Dad's voice in the evening, home from work.

When he was 17, Max moved in with a friend and worked at a grocery store to sustain himself—all to escape Dad's clutch. He returned only because Dad threatened to call the cops. But after he came home, Max confronted his father about his lousy parenting. Max Sr. had nothing to say.

Since the confrontation happened in full view of the family, his 11-year-old sister heard the just accusations Max filed against their father. A few months later, she spotted an apartment for rent while on her way home from school. The girl packed Mom's suitcase, took her younger brother, and convinced Mom to rent the unit for them.

If a tween could be so motivated to leave behind her father and house, is it any surprise Max reacted to his death with zero regret? If anything, he felt relieved. Now there was no need to deal with him ever again!

As for the letter he received, Max resolved, "One day I'll frame it. The letter proves what a jerk he was."

PARTS AND MORE PARTS

Parts can exhibit a whole gamut of reactions in the face of loss. It is possible for you to feel and find parts we have not discussed here. What do you do then?

Focus on that part with an open heart. Listen to it. One of my all-time favorite quotes comes from Dr. David Augsburger, a distinguished figure in the field of pastoral care and counseling: "Being heard is so close to being loved that for the average person they are almost indistinguishable."[1]

What he meant was that people are impacted when we listen to them. But what is true for people often applies to parts too. So when you find a part you are curious about, listen to it wholeheartedly. Ask your parts, *Why do you feel this way about the loss I am facing?* Don't presume you already know the answer. When you ask them directly, parts can teach you what you might never have realized about your rich internal world.

Listen to every part you find. Note all its reasons for feeling the way it does. Doing so will propel your parts closer toward healing.

PHYSICAL SYMPTOMS

Grievous can mean causing physical suffering;[2] small wonder grieving affects your soul *and* body both.

If falling asleep has been hard, if you keep waking up and cannot reclaim sleep, or if you keep having nightmares, ask your internal world if any of your parts are responsible. If yes, ask another question: *Can you talk to me during daytime instead?* If you attend to their concerns when they bring it up, you will have a better chance of regaining a peaceful night of rest.

Dr. Alan Wolfelt directs the Center for Loss and Life Transition. He details the following as signs your body is grieving: "Muscle aches and pains, shortness of breath, feelings of emptiness in your stomach, tightness in your throat or chest, digestive problems, sensitivity to noise, heart palpitations, queasiness, nausea, headaches, increased allergy symptoms, changes in appetite, weight loss or gain, agitation, and generalized tension."[3] If any of these symptoms has been plaguing you, please seek help. Notice I did not specify *medical* help, although it is not because I disapprove of modern medicine. See your doctor if physical challenges persist.

But there is also another possibility at play. Parts can create or exacerbate issues in our body. The late Derek Scott, certified IFS therapist and author, noted exiled feelings often show up somatically—through the body.[4]

It pays to treat your body kindly. If you have been having headaches since your beloved passed away, for instance, focus on the spot where the ache originates. Send it compassion. This act alone could mitigate physical discomfort. You can also ask your internal system if the headache developed because a part's grief has been exiled. If so, befriend that exiled part, witness its pain, and ask if it would be willing to unburden. Once your protector parts permit these feelings to emerge, your body may naturally shed its physical symptoms.

HELPLESSNESS

There is a reason God instructs us, in both the Old and New Testaments, to care for widows (Exodus 22:22-24; Deuteronomy 14:29; 27:19; Isaiah 10:1-2; James 1:27; 1 Timothy 5:3). Widows tend to develop helplessness—especially in the early stages of loss.[5] But you do not have to be a widow to feel helpless. So if you find a helpless part in your inner system, befriend it. Really listen to what it feels helpless about. If the part is fretting about something outside your wheelhouse—like fixing a leaky toilet or comforting a colicky baby—flip through the Rolodex of your mind. Who in your world might have this skillset? Who might know someone who can help?

After a hiking accident killed author Clarissa Moll's husband, she feared the daunting task of parenting four young children alone.[6] But she has since discovered it does not take two parents to raise a child, but "a whole church." So she "enlisted good men to invest in [her] children's lives."[7]

Let's follow her example. Yes, people can maim us with their unsympathetic remarks. That is because many—Christians included—carry unidentified emotional baggage. Still, being seen and accepted by others in the midst of our pain is healing. Grief feels lighter when shared.

THE "AM I DOING THIS WRONG?" PART

Speaking of insensitive remarks, someone might think it is their noble duty to remind you, "Your loss happened some time back. Move on already." A part of you might take this comment to heart and wonder if there *is* something wrong with you. Why has your grief lasted this long?

Remember, mourning is a personal affair. Nobody has the right to dictate the pace you—or your parts—set. With apologies to William Blake for repurposing his phrase, "the greater the joy, the deeper the sorrow."[8] That is, the closer you were to the deceased, the greater your grief would be.

Ask your part if this explanation helps. If not, ask the part, *Why do you worry I might be grieving incorrectly?*

If your part assumes there is something wrong with you be-cause you are unfazed by the loss of your person—like Max at the top of this chapter—let it know there is likely an explanation. Ask it, *Can you allow me to be curious and discover the reason?*

Here is a bonus tip. If a part is worrying that you are grieving (or doing IFS) incorrectly, this could signify the presence of an inner critic. To calm the "am I doing this wrong?" part, show your critic the impact of its criticisms. Let it know it can lend you the most help by softening its reproaches.

WHEN TO SEEK THERAPY

Not everyone with an emotional need requires therapy. Metabolizing grief may be challenging, but many have successfully done so on their own, without the aid of any counselor. However, when you are dealing with complications, I strongly advise you to contact a psychologist or grief therapist. Get into therapy.

What kind of complications? Here are three categories.[9]

Trauma-related complications. You fit in this category if the death you are mourning happened unexpectedly, violently, or if the deceased was an authority figure (a parent, pastor, coach, and so on) who also abused you. Likewise, please seek therapy if you are grappling with multiple losses at once. This includes if childhood issues are still haunting you. For instance, if you were abandoned as a child but have yet to process the emotional impact of what happened, your current loss may provoke feelings of abandonment, which would make your grief more unbearable.

Traumatic responses like hypervigilance, flashbacks, intrusive thoughts, avoidance behavior (including the tendency to isolate yourself), and feelings of despair and hopelessness are best faced with the fortifying presence of a professional who has completed formal training in psychology.

Disenfranchised grief complications. Ken Doka coined this term to mean grief that is socially censured by society.[10] An example is someone who dated a married man who later died. If she hides her grief when her lover—who was also someone else's husband—died, her grief is disenfranchised. If you feel pressured to suppress your grief for fear of reproof, consider contacting a therapist.

Fragile emotional states. If you were highly dependent on the deceased, if you were already dealing with low self-esteem, or if you are an older person who is also isolated, please partner with a professional to lessen your grief load.

But there is another group of mourners I wish I could talk to in person. A significant loss can threaten to erase all reasons for living. If this describes you, in that the loss you are mourning is also evoking suicidal impulses, I urge you to seek professional care. Please. There is zero shame in reaching out for help to preserve your life.

You will get the opportunity to meet with your parts before this chapter ends. But if the prompts in the final Dipping Inside segment do not lead to unburdening your parts, the next healing step may involve finding an IFS therapist. Experience tells me living with unburdened parts is better.

I crave the same for you.

FACING THE FUTURE

As time progresses, new reasons to mourn may rap on your door. Birthdays, anniversaries, milestones, major holidays—even seemingly innocuous events may reignite sorrow. A veil of tears might distort your vision as your grandchild toddles around. *If only my husband could see his latest grandchild learn to walk.* Conversely, if your child died or went missing, the growth of other people's kids might activate strong reactions. Consider revisiting this book then.

It is also helpful to face significant dates with a ritual. According to Drs. Evan Imber-Black and Janine Roberts, "When healing rituals have not occurred, or have been insufficient to compete the grief processes, a person can remain stuck in the past or unable to move forward in meaningful ways."[11]

What kind of rituals? For ideas, consult your family, elders, and, of course, your own parts. This is what one of my clients does on a regular basis. Every year, Nina checks in with her internal system in anticipation of significant dates surrounding her mother's death. Since Nina never married, she moved in to care for Mom after her father died. The dutiful daughter has done numerous activities in honor of Mom's memory—from eating at the diner she liked, to watching *Gone with the Wind* (Mom's favorite movie), to buying peonies (Mom's favorite flower) to decorate her grave with.

But what if your loss had no exact date, like in the case of a missing soldier? Imber-Black and Roberts suggest gathering loved ones together on the date your person went missing. In the case of suicide or other losses imbued with shame, consider throwing an un-birthday party—a celebration of the person's life on a day that is *not* the person's birthday.

Christmas and Thanksgiving mark another major time to greet your parts with an extra embrace. Because society equates Christmastime with cheer, some parts might feel pressured to plaster on a peppy look. Likewise for Thanksgiving—for those of us in North America—since Thanksgiving typically gathers families around.

The glaring absence of family members who have passed on is bound to breed sorrow, especially the first time your family reunites. As such, please avail your parts of an additional dose of compassion around these annual markers. Face your loss. Vocalize how this year's holiday season is different because of grief.

Following a loss, living the abundant life (John 10:10) requires intentionality. It starts by making your parts a regular, well, part of your life. Talk to them the way you would a hurting friend.

Don't wait until a trigger flusters you before you scamper inward to calm parts down.

On that note, whenever you are triggered, it means a part feels a direct hit. Restore your equilibrium by finding out the part within your system that became activated. (Just ask inside.) Once you have an idea on the identity, focus on that part. Ask, *What happened? What triggered you?* Befriend, listen, witness its story. Use this same sequence anytime a trigger activates any part.

DIPPING INSIDE

Let's round up all the parts you met in this book and greet them all with warmth. Imagine being at a favorite place, whether indoor or outdoor, and invite your parts to sit around you. Picture a wide enough space to accommodate all of them.

Check how each part has been doing since your loss. Ask if there is more they need to tell you about their grief. If there are more than one takers, ask them not to overwhelm you. Encourage parts to take a number and await their turns, similar to when you shop at a deli.

Listen to each with an open heart and write down every need your parts present.

_____

_____

_____

_____

Do they feel you have truly understood their concerns?

_____

_____

Now, focus on your exiles. If they have turned down prior opportunities to unburden, ask if anything needs to happen before they can willingly release their burden. Write it down.

Once they are ready to unburden, ask them to find wherever they have stored the burden—body, mind, memory, feelings—and remove it. Choose how to eliminate the burden: burning, scattering to the wind, submerging in the sea, giving it to God, or something else.

How do your exiles feel? Don't be surprised if you feel lighter or happier. Jot down what you notice inside.

Now that your exiles unburdened, ask your protector parts if they also want to unburden. Lead them through the same process. How do they feel?

_____

_____

_____

_____

After the unburdening is complete, ask if your parts would like to invite essential qualities to help their journey. Write them down and breathe in these qualities.

_____

_____

_____

_____

Please check in with your parts on a regular basis. If you do so, you will help them stay unburdened.

_____

_____

_____

_____

How about sealing this time with a prayer? Let's pray something like, "Jesus, Isaiah 53 calls you a man of sorrows. I ask you, who are familiar with suffering, to walk with me in my grief. Help all my parts release their burden in the right time."

In Jesus' name, so be it.

Grieving Wholeheartedly Over Time

O UTWARDLY BUSY, INWARDLY GRIEVING.

This slogan describes my world as the sixth anniversary of my father's death is approaching. In the last three months I rotated from attending to my practice, packing, and then unpacking—the house we have been restoring is finally ready—to hunting for lost items I *knew* I saw somewhere recently, to stealing fleeting moments to write. My industrious parts juggled all of the above while acutely reflecting on my fatherless state.

James 1:2-4 exhorts us to "consider it pure joy, my brothers and sisters, whenever you face trials of many kinds, because you know that the testing of your faith produces perseverance. Let perseverance finish its work so that you may be mature and complete, not lacking anything." By no means have I attained full maturity. I can alphabetize the list of things I still lack. But because examining your grief every so often—especially on significant milestones, like the anniversary of your loss—is fitting, I do so today.

The struggles I faced have mellowed me into becoming less reactive. But does the world think so too? I check with the person who knows me best.

John's response comes immediately. "Oh, *absolutely.*"

My sweetheart usually weighs his answer well before vocalizing anything. His instantaneous response informs me the answer to my question must have been so obvious it requires no deliberation.

If my husband's and my assessments are correct, the maturing I have had to do after Papa's death has molded me to look more like him. After all, he consistently modeled calmness. But losing one parent also prompted me to be more present for my remaining parent; not just because I love my mother, but also because she is my dad's bride.

Still—how I wish he could enjoy the morning here, from our renovated living room, whistling at the chirping birds in the yard.

Just like he used to do when I was small.

YOUR GRIEVING PARTS NEED YOU

Life after loss leaves us with a couple of options, but only one is viable. Moses demonstrated how devastating the alternative is. To skip mourning is to risk your future.

No, the better option is to invite every part of your soul into a relationship, and help them accept their new reality. This is what it means to grieve wholeheartedly. When you relate to your parts on a regular basis, you are showing them you are still here with them, even though their special person or dream house is no longer. Dick Schwartz shared about the time a riptide pulled him into the open sea, prompting some of his parts to anticipate death. Dick let his frantic parts know, "We might die, but I'll be with you as we do."[1] After Dick promised to be with his parts to the end, they calmed down. He eventually swam safely back to shore.

There is no reason for your (or my) parts to respond differently than Dick's if we pledge our presence to them. Your Self is unique. You are the only person on earth who can promise never to abandon your parts—and then deliver.

WHOLEHEARTED GRIEVING: POSSIBILITIES

An outcome of wholehearted grieving is the ability to integrate your loss with the rest of your world. This concept can take on many different forms. If you had to bury your better half, for instance, you may eventually decide to repurpose both of your wedding rings into a pendant or a new ring altogether. This gesture signals your acceptance of being single again, even when you did not seek the status yourself.

For some families, naming a baby after a loved one who died is a way to honor the deceased. Nona's son, Drew, died from an overdose. But when her daughter—Drew's sister—gave birth to a girl, she decided to use his name for the newborn's middle name.[2]

Some bereaved individuals honor the lives they lost by wearing a portion of their ashes in a locket necklace. Others commit to a course of action like creating a podcast; writing poetry; launching nonprofits and businesses.

Davey Blackburn's pregnant wife was shot to death at their home. Davey had to grieve the double loss of his wife and their unborn baby while having to raise their firstborn alone. About a year later, Kristi started attending the church he pastored. They got married and started Nothing Is Wasted ministry.[3]

Two of Karim and Nancy Iskander's children were walking in the crosswalk when a speeding driver hit and killed them both. As a tribute to their slain boys, the Iskanders started a foundation to improve the lives of underserved children worldwide.[4]

After Kate's husband died, her sister prepared a present with strict instructions. Kate was only to open the gift when facing a tough day. The healing power of that experience compelled both women to replicate the idea through Rainy Day Boxes, where givers can send a curated box of gifts for mourners.[5]

But perhaps you do not have an entrepreneurial mindset or wish to publicize your story. This is fine. There is no chapter or verse mandating you to champion a cause after suffering a loss. Grieving with your whole heart can simply translate into hoping again; not hiding from the future because it may elicit more losses, but pursuing God's dreams for you with an open heart.

FEAR AND GREAT JOY

Mary Magdalene had reasons to mourn. After Jesus expelled all seven demons from her, Mary became a faithful follower. She witnessed the miracles he performed, listened to his sermons, and traveled with the rest of the disciples as he taught the gospel from town to town (Luke 8:1-3). She even stomached the agony of witnessing her teacher's prolonged execution (Mark 15:40-41) and lingered until they buried his body (Mark 15:47). This turn of events must have deeply grieved her.

What next?

She and a friend decided to pay a visit to the grave of their deceased. But they arrived to a startling sight: instead of Jesus' body, an angel awaited them with news that Jesus had risen from the dead (Matthew 28:1-7).

Notice how they respond to this staggering news: "They went out quickly from the tomb with *fear and great joy*, and ran to bring his disciples word" (Matthew 28:8 NKJV, italics added). Most other translations agree; their joy surpassed their fear.

Fear and *great* joy.

This phrase portrays the essence of wholehearted grieving. Years after your loss, no matter how diligent you are in helping them unburden, your parts may still carry residues of remorse. Or pain. Maybe fear. Sadness is like a mangosteen stain, remember? Although your future sorrow may not feel as intense, if the loss that took you to this book *is* considerable, it will etch your soul with a permanent mark.

Then again, that marker will not saturate your entire system. When you regularly support your parts, they will eventually unburden their grief, liberating mental resources you can draw on to engage life earnestly. You will never forget those who departed your world, of course—but neither will you let loss define your entire existence.

Paul exhorted us to "keep focused on that goal, those of us who want everything God has for us" (Philippians 3:15 MSG). As you nurture your present relationships, the strength of your shared bond can empower you to keep going—until you reach all God has intended for you.

Your own promised land, so to speak.

A HEARTFELT GOODBYE

Before we close, let's revisit Mary Magdalene. We saw how she hurried from the tomb fearful—but bubbling with great joy, courtesy of the angel's message. Jesus was alive *and* available. For her! This detail is worth highlighting, because—as we have seen throughout this book—goodbyes are hard.

But since the reliable presence of someone kind can ease the pain of separation, as we finish our time together, let me refer you to the One who has vowed to stay, even when everyone else departs. God has promised, "Never will I leave you; never will I forsake you" (Hebrews 13:5).

Thank you for journeying with me. I am grateful for you and your parts. May they find healing in your presence—and the Lord's.

Acknowledgments

LORD JESUS, I HAVE MORE GRATITUDE than space allows, but you know (and have) my heart. Thank you for making the impossible happen time and again. The glory is forever yours.

John, being married to you is like living with a biological billboard of 1 Corinthians 13. I love you. Thank you for your unwavering support.

Mama, what have I *not* inherited from you? Everything from faith to fashion sense I obtained because I'm your daughter. Thank you for your sacrifices. Audrey sayang mama.

To the entire Lim clan, I'm honored to share your lineage.

CHURCH FAMILY

Michael and Helena's connect group has lent me much emotional and spiritual support throughout the entire publishing ordeal. You supported me throughout, starting from when this book was a mere wisp of an idea. You guys are very dear to my heart.

What an honor it is to uplift prayer after prayer with the dedicated team of intercessors at church! Pastor Mando, Lynette, Gene, and the Tuesday morning/Wednesday afternoon prayer warriors, you're my kind of people.

To the 2023 Marrieds Class couples, *so* glad for the friendships we've developed!

IFS TRIBE

Jeff and Martha, I love being a part of JAM with you. Let's keep growing in IFS together, shall we? And Jenny, thanks for squeezing our consultation needs into your busy schedule.

Dick, thank you for being a conduit for this exceptional therapy modality. I love you and Jeanne both. I learned a ton from the trainers I've PA'ed for—but especially Chris, my consultant for years.

Shout out to fellow PA's I've met along the way!

WRITING CREW

Karen, I'll never forget how you agreed to represent me before my platform looked presentable. Thank you for believing in me.

Al, thank you for lending your expertise to improve this book. To the rest of the team at InterVarsity Press, I appreciate every one of you.

I'm thankful for every writer, author, and editor who has sharpened my writing over the years.

At the Dream Center Counseling Center, Moriah Heizer typed into a digital file paragraphs I had highlighted in the hard copies I read. Her industriousness eased my writing process, for which I'm grateful.

ANONYMOUS CLIENTS

As a psychologist, I'm restricted from identifying those who willingly bared their souls to me. So, to all my clients, even though I can't credit you by name, know that I cherish you and your parts. Thank you for trusting me. I don't take for granted the access you afforded me into your internal world.

Notes

INTRODUCTION

[1]*Inside Out*, directed by Pete Doctor (Emeryville, CA: Pixar Animation Studio, 2015) and *Inside Out 2*, directed by Kelsey Mann (Emeryville, CA: Pixar Animation Studio, 2024). These animated movies feature Riley and her major emotions. If you wish to learn how *Inside Out 2* reflects IFS principles, see Audrey Davidheiser, "Inside Out 2 & IFS," Aim for Breakthrough, accessed November 4, 2024, www.aimforbreakthrough.com/inside-out-2/.

1. GRIEVING

[1]Elizabeth Kübler-Ross, *On Death and Dying* (New York: Scribner, 1970).

[2]Elizabeth Kübler-Ross and David Kessler, *On Grief and Grieving* (New York: Scribner, 2005), 7.

[3]Mary Lamia, *Grief Isn't Something to Get Over* (Washington, DC: American Psychological Association, 2022).

[4]John R. Jordan, "Lessons Learned: Forty Years of Clinical Work with Suicide Loss Survivors," *Frontiers in Psychology, 11*, no. 1-9 (April 2020): www.frontiersin.org/journals/psychology/articles/10.3389/fpsyg.2020.00766/full.

[5]Elyce Wakerman, *Father Loss: Daughters Discuss Life, Love, and Why Losing a Dad Means So Much* (New York: Yucca, 2015), chap. 3, Kindle.

[6]Toni Miles, et al., "Estimating Prevalence of Bereavement, Its Contribution to Risk for Binge Drinking, and Other High-Risk Health States in a State Population Survey, 2019 Georgia Behavioral Risk Factor Surveillance Survey," May 2023, https://doi.org/10.3390/ijerph20105837.

[7]Jim Windell, "The Hidden Cost of Grief," Michigan Psychological Association, accessed October 18, 2024, www.michiganpsychologicalassociation.org/index.php?option=com_dailyplanetblog&view=entry&category=covid19&id=139%3Athe-hidden-cost-of-grief.

2. THE ABCS OF IFS

[1]Richard C. Schwartz, *Internal Family Systems Therapy* (New York: Guilford Press, 1995).

[2]Martha Sweezy and Ellen L. Ziskind, *Internal Family Systems Therapy: New Dimensions* (New York: Routledge, 2013).

[3]Hilary B. Hodgdon et al., "Internal Family Systems (IFS) Therapy for Posttraumatic Stress Disorder (PTSD) Among Survivors of Multiple Childhood Trauma: A Pilot Effectiveness Study," *Journal of Aggression, Maltreatment & Trauma 31*, no. 1 (December 27, 2021): 22-43, www.tandfonline.com/doi/full/10.1080/10926771.2021.2013375.

[4]Richard C. Schwartz and Martha Sweezy, *Internal Family Systems Therapy*, 2nd ed. (New York: Guilford Press, 2020).

[5]Richard C. Schwartz, *No Bad Parts: Healing Trauma and Restoring Wholeness with the Internal Family Systems Model* (Louisville, CO: Sounds True, 2021), chap. 1, Kindle.

[6]Martha Sweezy, *Internal Family Systems for Shame and Guilt* (New York: Guilford Press, 2023).

[7]Frank Anderson, *Transcending Trauma: Healing Complex PTSD with Internal Family Systems* (Eau Claire, WI: PESI Publishing, 2021), chap. 1, Kindle.

[8]J. William Worden, *Grief Counseling and Grief Therapy, Fourth Edition: A Handbook for the Mental Health Practitioner* (New York: Springer Publishing, 2009).

[9]Schwartz, *No Bad Parts*, chap. 2, Kindle.

[10]"The 8 C's of Self Leadership Wheel," Foundation IFS, accessed November 4, 2024, https://foundationifs.org/images/banners/pdf/The_8_Cs_of_Self_Leadership_Wheel.pdf.

[11]Christopher L. Heuertz, *The Sacred Enneagram: Finding Your Unique Path to Spiritual Growth* (Grand Rapids, MI: Zondervan, 2017).

[12]Heuertz, *The Sacred Enneagram*, 28.

[13]Heuertz, *The Sacred Enneagram*. According to Heuertz, there are a few different labels people have assigned to Enneagram types. The ones listed here are from the Enneagram Institute, www.enneagraminstitute.com/type-descriptions/.

[14]Joan Ryan and Tammy Sollenberger, "IFS and the Enneagram: Connecting to Parts Using the Enneagram Map," in *Altogether Us: Integrating the IFS Model with Key Modalities, Communities, and Trends*, ed. Jenna Riemersma (Pivotal Press, 2023), chap. 25, Kindle.

[15]Schwartz and Sweezy, *Internal Family Systems Therapy*.

3. IFS AND CHRISTIAN FAITH

[1]I credit Jeff Wallace as the first colleague who informed me of these comparisons.

[2]Joseph Bayly, *The View from a Hearse* (Bloomington, IN: Warhorn Publishing, 2014), chap. 9, Kindle.

[3]Jack Hayford, *Rebuilding The Real You: The Definitive Guide to the Holy Spirit's Work in Your Life* (Lake Mary, FL: Charisma Media, 2013), 40.

[4]Witness Lee, "Dealing with Our Inward Parts for the Growth in Life," Living Stream Ministry, accessed October 21, 2024, www.ministrysamples.org /excerpts/THE-SOUL-HAVING-THREE-PARTS.html.

[5]Another evidence of patterns in creation comes in the form of numbers. The same numbers repeat throughout Scripture. If you take forty, for example, the children of Israel wandered the wilderness for forty years (Joshua 5:6); Moses fasted for forty days and nights (Exodus 24:18, 34:28); Jesus did too (Matthew 4:2); a number of judges and kings ruled Israel for forty years apiece—like Eli (1 Samuel 4:18), Othniel (Judges 3:11), David (2 Samuel 5:4, 1 Kings 2:11), and his son Solomon (1 Kings 11:42).

[6]My deep gratitude goes to members of the Christian IFS Facebook group for alerting me to Psalm 103:1 (Karon Ng) and Isaiah 61:1 (Matt Evans). For the Hebrew meaning of the word *brokenhearted*, see https://biblehub.com /hebrew/7665.htm.

[7]The person I first learned this concept from is Kenneth J. Doka, *Grief Is a Journey: Finding Your Path Through Loss* (New York: Atria Books, 2016), chap. 1, Kindle.

[8]Richard C. Schwartz, *No Bad Parts: Healing Trauma and Restoring Wholeness with the Internal Family Systems Model* (Louisville, CO: Sounds True, 2021), Kindle, chap. 5.

4. PLENTY OF PERMISSION

[1]Kenneth J. Doka, *Grief Is a Journey: Finding Your Path Through Loss* (New York: Atria Books, 2016), chap. 1, Kindle.

[2]Jerry Sittser, *A Grace Disguised: How the Soul Grows Through Loss* (Grand Rapids, MI: Zondervan, 2021), chap. 6, Kindle.

[3]Doka, *Grief Is a Journey*, chap. 1, Kindle.

5. TWO COMMON MANAGERS

[1]Dallas Jenkins, "Binge Jesus Isn't Really About *The Chosen*," www.youtube .com/watch?v=-gdenpbKXpE, accessed July 29, 2024.

[2]Richard C. Schwartz and Martha Sweezy, *Internal Family Systems Therapy*, 2nd ed. (New York: Guilford Press, 2020), 33.

[3]Marc Brackett, *Permission to Feel: Unlocking the Power of Emotions to Help Our Kids, Ourselves, and Our Society Thrive* (New York: Celadon Books, 2010), 13.

[4]J. William Worden, *Grief Counseling and Grief Therapy: A Handbook for the Mental Health Practitioner*, 4th ed. (New York: Springer Publishing, 2009).

[5]Richard C. Schwartz, *Internal Family Systems Therapy* (New York: Guilford Press, 1995).

[6]C. S. Lewis, *A Grief Observed* (San Francisco, CA: HarperOne, 1961), 10.

[7]Kenneth J. Doka, *Grief Is a Journey: Finding Your Path Through Loss* (New York: Atria Books, 2016), Kindle.

[8]Doka, *Grief Is a Journey*, chap. 4, Kindle.

[9]Chris Burris, Senior Lead Trainer at the IFS Institute, personal communication.

[10]Cece Sykes, Senior Lead Trainer at the IFS Institute, personal communication.

6. YOUR MOST RELIGIOUS PART

[1]Steve Shermett, "The Smiling Pharisees. *The Chosen's* Rabbis Akiva and Josiah Zoom Chat," accessed November 4, 2024, www.youtube.com/watch?v=_bg1XjeZnIg.

[2]"*The Chosen*, 'Not All Pharisees Are Bad Guys,'" accessed November 4, 2024, www.youtube.com/watch?v=R6gat-FZ7ME.

[3]"choli," *Strong's Concordance*, accessed October 25, 2024, https://biblehub.com/hebrew/2483.htm.

[4]"makob," Strong's Concordance, accessed October 25, 2024, https://biblehub.com/hebrew/4341.htm.

7. FIREFIGHTERS

[1]Fiona Ng, "The One Where We Lost A Friend: Fans React to Matthew Perry's Passing," LAist, October 29, 2023. https://laist.com/news/arts-and-entertainment/the-one-where-we-lost-a-friend-fans-react-to-matthew-perrys-passing.

[2]Todd Spangler, "*Friends* Shoots to Top of TV Streaming Charts Following Matthew Perry's Death," *Variety*, November 7, 2023, https://variety.com/2023/digital/news/friends-top-streaming-charts-matthew-perry-1235782772/.

[3]J. William Worden, *Grief Counseling and Grief Therapy: A Handbook for the Mental Health Practitioner*, 4th ed. (New York: Springer Publishing, 2009).

[4]Lisa Shulman, *Before and After Loss: A Neurologist's Perspective on Loss, Grief, and Our Brain* (Baltimore, MD: Johns Hopkins University Press, 2018), 132.

[5]Matthew Perry, *Friends, Lovers, and the Big Terrible Thing: A Memoir* (New York: Flatiron Books, 2022), Kindle iOS version.

[6]Sarah Hepola, "Matthew Perry's Radical Honesty About His Addiction Battle Helped Us All," *Rolling Stone*, October 31, 2023, www.rollingstone

.com/tv-movies/tv-movie-features/matthew-perry-drug-addiction-honesty
-friends-memoir-rehab-1234866429/.

[7]Matthew Perry (@MatthewPerry), "Extremely skilled poet and dancer with
a seemingly endless sense of longing. Hi!," Twitter (X), accessed October 25,
2024, https://twitter.com/MatthewPerry.

[8]Jeannie Ortega Law, "Matthew Perry Recounted Encounter with the 'Presence
of God' in His Book Before Death," *Christian Post*, November 1, 2023, www
.christianpost.com/news/matthew-perry-recounted-his-encounter-with-the
-presence-of-god.html.

[9]Holly Yan and Jay Croft, "How Doctors and a 'Ketamine Queen' Took Ad-
vantage of Matthew Perry and Played a Role in His Death, According to Pros-
ecutors," *CNN*, August 18, 2024, www.cnn.com/2024/08/16/entertainment
/matthew-perry-suspects-took-advantage.

[10]Christopher L. Heuertz, *The Sacred Enneagram: Finding Your Unique Path to
Spiritual Growth* (Grand Rapids, MI: Zondervan, 2017), 22.

8. SHOCK

[1]*Pempek*: A fish cake dish from the South Sumatra province in Indonesia. Made
of tapioca flour and ground fish meat, *pempek* can be fried or boiled. It is best
consumed with a sauce that is altogether sweet, sour, and spicy.

[2]Mary-Frances O'Connor, *The Grieving Brain: The Surprising Science of How We
Learn from Love and Loss* (New York: Harper One, 2022), 49.

[3]A. Pawlowski, "The Grieving Brain: How Your Mind Deals with a Loved One's
Death and How To Heal," *Today*, January 26, 2022, www.today.com/health
/mind-body/grief-changes-brain-rcna13613.

9. SADNESS AND SORROW

[1]J. William Worden, *Grief Counseling and Grief Therapy: A Handbook for the
Mental Health Practitioner*, 4th ed. (New York: Springer Publishing, 2009).

[2]Francis Weller, *The Wild Edge of Sorrow: Rituals of Renewal and the Sacred Work
of Grief* (Berkeley, CA: North Atlantic Books, 2015), chap. 3, Kindle.

[3]C. S. Lewis, *A Grief Observed* (San Francisco, CA: Harper One, 1961), 53.

[4]Mary Lamia, *Grief Isn't Something to Get Over* (Washington, DC: American Psychological Association, 2022).

10. ANGER AND RAGE

[1]John Townsend, *Hiding from Love* (Grand Rapids, MI: Zondervan, 1996), 96.

[2]Brené Brown, *Atlas of the Heart: Mapping Meaningful Connection and the Language of Human Experience* (New York: Random House, 2021).

[3]ABC News, "Are You Angry at God?," December 21, 2010, *ABC News*, https://abcnews.go.com/Technology/angry-god-thirds-americans-blame-god-problems-survey/story?id=12540557.

[4]Megan Brenan, "Americans' Mental Health Ratings Sink to New Low," *Gallup*, December 7, 2020, https://news.gallup.com/poll/327311/americans-mental-health-ratings-sink-new-low.aspx.

[5]Joanne H. Twombly, *Trauma and Dissociation Informed Internal Family Systems: How to Successfully Treat C-PTSD, and Dissociative Disorders* (self-published, 2022), Kindle iOS version.

11. GUILT AND REGRET

[1]Rita Schulte, *Surviving Suicide Loss: Making Your Way Beyond the Ruins* (Chicago: Northfield Publishing, 2021), chap. 1, Kindle.

[2]Kenneth J. Doka, *Grief Is a Journey: Finding Your Path Through Loss* (New York: Atria Books, 2016).

[3]J. William Worden, *Grief Counseling and Grief Therapy: A Handbook for the Mental Health Practitioner* (New York: Springer Publishing, 2009).

[4]Schulte, *Surviving Suicide Loss*, chap. 5.

[5]Iain Provan, in Casey B. Hough, *Known for Love* (Chicago: Moody Publishers, 2024), chap. 1, Kindle.

12. FEAR

[1]Elyce Wakerman, *Father Loss: Daughters Discuss Life, Love, and Why Losing a Dad Means So Much* (New York: Yucca, 2015), chap. 10, Kindle.

[2]J. William Worden, *Grief Counseling and Grief Therapy: A Handbook for the Mental Health Practitioner*, 4th ed. (New York: Springer Publishing, 2009).

[3]C. S. Lewis, foreword to *A Grief Observed* (San Francisco, CA: HarperOne, 1961).

[4]Ken Doka, "Grief in the COVID-19 Pandemic," in *Death, Grief and Loss in the Context of COVID-19*, ed. Panagiotis Pentaris (London: Routledge, 2022), 29-39.

[5]Doka, "Grief in the COVID-19 Pandemic," 30-31.

[6]"habituation," *APA Dictionary of Psychology*, accessed October 29, 2024, https://dictionary.apa.org/habituation.

[7]Susan David, "The Gift and Power of Emotional Courage," TEDWomen, November 2017, 16:38, www.ted.com/talks/susan_david_the_gift_and_power_of_emotional_courage/.

[8]J. Alasdair Groves and Winston T. Smith, *Untangling Emotions: God's Gift of Emotions* (Wheaton, IL: Crossway, 2019), chap. 13, Kindle.

[9]Frank Anderson, *Transcending Trauma: Healing Complex PTSD with Internal Family Systems* (Eau Claire, WI: PESI Publishing, 2021).

[10]"sozo: to save," Strong's concordance, accessed October 29, 2024, https://biblehub.com/greek/4982.htm.

13. LONELINESS AND ISOLATION

[1]Tad Friend, "Jumpers," *The New Yorker*, October 5, 2003, www.newyorker.com/magazine/2003/10/13/jumpers.

[2]Brené Brown, *Atlas of the Heart: Mapping Meaningful Connection and the Language of Human Experience* (New York: Random House, 2021).

[3]Eric Marcus, *Why Suicide? Answers to 200 of the Most Frequently Asked Questions About Suicide, Attempted Suicide, and Assisted Suicide* (San Francisco: HarperCollins, 1996), 21.

[4]Theo Boer and Kevin Yuill, "Assisted Dying and COVID-19," in *Death, Grief and Loss in the Context of COVID-19*, ed. P. Pentaris (New York: Routledge, 2022), 186.

[5]Boer and Yuill, "Assisted Dying and COVID-19," 191.

[6]Boer and Yuill, "Assisted Dying and COVID-19."

[7]Brown, *Atlas of the Heart*, 180.

[8]C. M. Masi et al., "A Meta-Analysis of Interventions to Reduce Loneliness," *Personality and Social Psychology Review* 15, (2011): https://doi.org/10.1177/1088868310377394.

[9]Masi, et al., "A Meta-Analysis of Interventions to Reduce Loneliness."

[10]Brown, *Atlas of the Heart*, 179.

14. OTHER POSSIBLE PARTS

[1]David Augsburger, *Caring Enough To Hear and Be Heard* (Ventura, CA: Regal Books, 1982), 12.

[2]Alan D. Wolfelt and Kirby J. Duvall, *Healing Your Grieving Body: 100 Practical Practices for Mourners* (Fort Collins, CO: Companion Press, 2009).

[3]Wolfelt and Duvall, introduction to *Healing Your Grieving Body*.

[4]Derek Scott, "Self-led Grieving," in *Innovations and Elaborations in Internal Family Systems Therapy*, eds. Martha Sweezy and Ellen L. Ziskind (New York: Taylor & Francis, 2017), 107.

[5]J. William Worden, *Grief Counseling and Grief Therapy: A Handbook for the Mental Health Practitioner* (New York: Springer Publishing, 2009).

[6]Clarissa Moll, *Beyond the Darkness: A Gentle Guide for Living with Grief & Thriving After Loss* (Carol Stream, IL: Tyndale, 2022).

[7]Clarissa Moll (@mollclarissa), "I've been solo parenting for 4.5 years since my husband's death, and I can tell you one thing for sure," Instagram, January 26, 2024, www.instagram.com/p/C2kgUHfLILR/.

[8]The actual quote is the opposite: "The deeper the sorrow, the greater the joy." Francis Weller, *The Wild Edge of Sorrow: Rituals of Renewal and the Sacred Work of Grief* (Berkeley, CA: North Atlantic Books, 2015), chap. 8, Kindle.

[9]I culled these categories from J. William Worden, *Grief Counseling and Grief Therapy: A Handbook for the Mental Health Practitioner*, 4th ed. (New York, Springer Publishing, 2009).

[10]Kenneth J. Doka, *Grief Is a Journey: Finding Your Path Through Loss* (New York: Atria Books, 2016).

[11]Evan Imber-Black and Janine Roberts, *Rituals for our Times: Celebrating, Healing, and Changing Our Lives and Our Relationships* (New York: Harper-Collins Publishers, 1992), 40.

15. GRIEVING WHOLEHEARTEDLY OVER TIME

[1]Richard C. Schwartz, *No Bad Parts: Healing Trauma and Restoring Wholeness with the Internal Family Systems Model* (Louisville, CO: Sounds True, 2021), chap. 7, Kindle.

[2]"Nona Perdue," Speaking Grief, accessed November 4, 2024, https://speaking grief.org/stories-of-grief/nona-perdue.

[3]Nothing Is Wasted, website, accessed November 4, 2024, www.nothing iswasted.com/our-story.

[4]Sid Garcia, "'Part of Me Is Dead': Nancy Iskander Disappointed in Grossman Sentence, Apology," ABC 7, June 20, 2024, https://abc7.com/post/nancy -iskander-mother-boys-killed-socialite-rebecca-grossman-westlake-village /14941498/.

[5]"Our Story," Rainy Day Boxes, accessed November 4, 2024, https://rainyday boxes.com/pages/our-story/.

About the Author

AUDREY DAVIDHEISER, PhD, is a California-licensed psychologist, certified Internal Family Systems (IFS) therapist, and IFSI-approved clinical consultant. After founding and directing a counseling center for the Los Angeles Dream Center, she now devotes her practice to survivors of trauma—including spiritual abuse. Visit her on www.aimforbreakthrough.com and Instagram @DrAudreyD.

Like this book?
Scan the code to discover more content like this!

Get on IVP's email list to receive special offers, exclusive book news, and thoughtful content from your favorite authors on topics you care about.

ivp | InterVarsity Press